"As an adjunct apologist with Ravi Zacharias International Ministries, Alex McLellan is a tremendous asset to our international speaking team. His writing is equally compelling, for he shows how metaphor and real-life stories make sense of the gospel for skeptics and believers alike. I wholeheartedly recommend this book."

RAVI ZACHARIAS, author and speaker

"Alex has a passion for communicating ultimate truth to ordinary people. This book is a powerful resource for Christians who want to share their faith with confidence, and to those still seeking answers."

JOSH D. MCDOWELL, author and speaker

"This is a warm, well-informed, conversational approach to worldview issues. McLellan presents an effective cumulative-case strategy for making sense out of life by navigating the waters of competing world-views. Readers will be strengthened in their faith and equipped to share that faith with others."

J. P. MORELAND, Distinguished Professor of Philosophy, Talbot School of Theology, and author of *The God Question*

"When the world around you seems confusing and disoriented, it's important to find a way to make sense of it all. My friend Alex McLellan may just be the one you're looking for. His insightful treatment of the world from God's point of view is a compelling tool to help you navigate through the confusion by taking you to God and his Word."

JOSEPH M. STOWELL, president, Cornerstone University, Grand Rapids, Michigan

"Alex McLellan's book is a thoughtful, practical guide to making sense of the world. McLellan is culturally astute, but he makes his observations accessible and his points memorable for a popular audience."

PAUL COPAN, professor and Pledger Family Chair of Philosophy and Ethics, Palm Beach Atlantic University

"Defending the faith in a hostile world is sorely needed as increasing numbers aim their weapons at Christianity and the Bible. McLellan's *Jigsaw Guide* provides another valuable tool for the believer who is serious about engaging with the worldview of postmodern culture. Read, digest and help others make sense of the world."

J. PAUL NYQUIST, PH.D., president, Moody Bible Institute

"Alex McLellan makes a winsome case for 'confident Christianity,' which results from the belief that we can know the truth without knowing everything. But he doesn't stop there, and neither should you. He shows how knowing the truth compels us to share the gospel with a broken world and offer those in our spheres of influence the wholeness found in Christ alone."

BARRY H. COREY, president, Biola University

"Defending the faith has never been more practical. From allusions to James Bond to citations from scientists and philosophers, from the classroom to the real world, Alex McLellan guides readers over, around and through current obstacles to effective witness in the arena of ideas. The strategy developed here is wise and liberating. You'll be looking forward to his next book, or booking him to speak for your next event."

R. DOUGLAS GEIVETT, Talbot Department of Philosophy, Biola University

A Jigsaw Guide
to Making Sense
of the World

Alex McLellan

IVP Books

An imprint of InterVarsity Press
Downers Grove, Illinois

InterVarsity Press
P.O. Box 1400, Downers Grove, IL 60515-1426
World Wide Web: www.ivpress.com
E-mail: email@ivpress.com

InterVarsity Press® is the book-publishing division of InterVarsity Christian Fellowship/USA®, a
movement of students and faculty active on campus at hundreds of universities, colleges and schools
of nursing in the United States of America, and a member movement of the International Fellowship
of Evangelical Students. For information about local and regional activities, write Public Relations
Dept., InterVarsity Christian Fellowship/USA, 6400 Schroeder Rd., P.O. Box 7895, Madison, WI
53707-7895, or visit the IVCF website at <www.intervarsity.org>.

All Scripture quotations, unless otherwise indicated, are taken from the Holy Bible, New
International Version®. NIV®. Copyright ©1973, 1978, 1984 by International Bible Society. Used by
permission of Zondervan Publishing House. All rights reserved.

While all stories in this book are true, some names and identifying information in this book have
been changed to protect the privacy of the individuals involved.

(other permissions needed):

Design: Cindy Kiple
Interior Design: Beth Hagenberg
Images: jigsaw puzzle: ©lilly3/iStock
       blue jigsaw puzzle: ©kyoshino/iStockphoto
       puzzle pieces: ©Alex Slobodkin/iStockphoto

ISBN 978-0-8308-3781-6

Printed in the United States of America ∞

Library of Congress Cataloging-in-Publication Data has been requested.

P	15	14	13	12	11	10	9	8	7	6	5	4	3	2	1
Y	22	21	20	19	18	17	16	15	14	13	12				

Dedicated to Sheryl

my wife,
my partner in life,
my partner in ministry,
my best friend

If I am asked the purely intellectual question,
why I believe in Christianity, I can only answer . . .
I believe in it quite rationally upon the evidence.
But the evidence in my case . . . is in an enormous
accumulation of small but unanimous facts.

G. K. Chesterton, Orthodoxy

CONTENTS

Introduction / 11
Seeing the Big Picture

1 Jigsaw / 19
Be Prepared to See It

2 Truth / 54
Be Prepared to Handle It

3 Belief / 80
Be Prepared to Share It

4 Faith / 102
Be Prepared to Anchor It

5 Doubt / 124
Be Prepared to Deal with It

6 The Big Picture / 144
Be Prepared to Show It

Acknowledgements / 179

Notes / 183

INTRODUCTION

Seeing the Big Picture

My eldest daughter used to love doing jigsaws as a young girl, and one day I spoke to her about a puzzle she was working on. "Sophia, I wonder what the picture is?" She confidently responded, "Dad, it's Cinderella!" I recognized a teachable moment and pointed out, "But you haven't put all the pieces together." She merely tilted her head and said, "Dad, it's Cinderella!"

I faked a serious expression and challenged her again, this time with more emotion. "Sophia, wait, it's not too late to change your mind. You can't be sure because you haven't completed the puzzle." Sophia, who is used to her dad asking unusual questions, merely rolled her eyes the way only a daughter can. "Dad, it's Cinderella and I'm sure because I have enough pieces in place."

Clearly Sophia had seen the box and retained this picture in her mind. In fact, it would be easy to assume this was what she was referring to when I asked her about the big picture. But note what she said: "Dad, I have enough pieces in place." Sophia's attention had shifted from the box to the puzzle pieces. These were now responsible for her confidence about the big picture. My daughter had stumbled on something significant about this broken world, and I wanted to be sure she remembered it: We can know the truth—and we can know the truth without knowing everything.

I have lost count of the number of times a meaningful conversation has ground to a halt when someone shrugged his or her shoulders and said, "Well, we can't really know because we'll never have all the answers." I normally agree that we'll never find every answer to every question, but I like to get the conversation back on track. Many people look at this broken world and think we can't make sense of it all. However, like when we're doing a jigsaw, if we want to see the big picture we don't need every piece of a puzzle. All we need is enough important parts that stand out and fit together.

Don't be put off by things in life that don't make sense or stumped by parts that don't seem to fit. Turn your attention to what clearly stands out and start snapping things into place. While it can be frustrating to know we'll never complete this puzzle, it's worth the effort to try to see the big picture. When you've done enough to see enough, you'll be confident you know the truth.

This is a jigsaw guide to making sense of the world, and it is a strategy that comes naturally. Transcending boundaries of age, language, intellect and culture, the jigsaw idea has connected with people around the world, and we can use it everywhere to talk about things that really matter. I've stood before the Scottish Parliament and used the jigsaw to make a cumulative case for the truth and reasonableness of the Christian worldview. When you hold this key to confident Christianity, you are prepared to share anywhere!

For a long time I've known that Christianity is more than endorsing tradition or subscribing to a religion because it offers a unique relationship with God that changes lives. I learned this firsthand as a young boy growing up in Edinburgh, Scotland. My parents, Alex and June McLellan, were unchurched and non-Christian. By the time I was three years old, my sister Paula and I joined the long list of children whose families had been fragmented by divorce. However, a few years later my parents became Christians, radically changed for the better and decided to get remarried—to each other. Witnessing this transformation got my attention and encouraged me to commit my life to Jesus Christ.

If Christianity is real, change is important, but I came to understand that change is not enough. The ultimate question is not "does it work?" but "is it true?" In my teenage years I wrestled with this question until an absence of answers made it easier to drift away from God, and this steady slide continued until difficult circumstances drew me back to faith. The sharp edges of life remind us that we cannot put off until tomorrow what we need to do today. I knew I had to decide where I stood in relation to God and his Son, Jesus Christ. I needed to switch my attention from the missing pieces of the puzzle to what I believed about the big picture. I realized my faith still stood—and stood strong—because it rang true. Therefore I was responsible to do something about it, and I wholeheartedly recommitted my life to Christ.

C. S. Lewis, one of the most influential Christian writers of the twentieth century, said, "If you examined a hundred people who had lost their faith in Christianity, I wonder how many of them would turn out to have been reasoned out of it by honest argument? Do not most people simply drift away?"[1] I knew the danger of this, so I was determined to do whatever it took to strengthen my belief and add weight to the anchor in my soul: to know what I believed and the reasons I believed it. This was the first step on a lifelong journey. I knew I needed God's help, so like the man in Mark's Gospel I prayed, "[Lord,] I do believe; help me overcome my unbelief!" (Mk 9:24).

Today I am the founder and executive director of Reason Why International, traveling broadly to speak at churches, universities, schools, camps, conferences and a variety of outreach events and sharing the good news of Jesus Christ. What changed? My overwhelming conviction that Christianity is true! How did this happen? I was not zapped by a supernatural bolt of under-standing. Rather, I learned many good reasons to believe that a biblical perspective provides the right framework for life and resonates with reality.

James Sire is a respected author and authority on worldviews, and he describes a worldview as "a set of presuppositions (assumptions which may be true, partly true or entirely false) which we hold (consciously or subconsciously, consistently or inconsistently) about the basic make-up of our world."[2] So when I had good reasons to believe that the Christian worldview corresponded to the real world, it strengthened my faith and gave me renewed confidence in the gospel. Christianity fits! *A Jigsaw Guide to Making Sense of the World* is designed to help believers see and appreciate this, and every reason to believe it fits is a reason to share.

While reasons to believe you know the truth can provide confidence, it's still not easy for Christians to stand up, open their mouths and share the Christian faith, especially when it seems like the world is telling them to sit down, be quiet and keep their beliefs to themselves. This leads us to think things like, "I can't share the truth about Christianity because people get offended." "People say everyone should be left alone to believe what they want." "My faith is rejected as out of touch with the real world." "If I open the door to doubt it will destroy my faith." These kinds of obstacles can erode confidence in the gospel and suck the life out of our passion for evangelism. So when it comes to sharing their faith, many Christians default to the school of "I would if I could, but I can't!"

If Christians see themselves as not smart enough, bold enough or gifted enough, they can withdraw from conversations and take the fallback position: live right and let their actions speak for themselves. This may seem like a good idea until it becomes obvious that a silent Christian example often leads only to one conclusion: "What a nice person." The other problem with handing over responsibility to those more "qualified" is that the Bible hands it right back. All Christians need to be ready to share what they believe and why they believe it (1 Pet 3:15). When we share those reasons, whether or not we realize it we are participating in Christian apologetics. There are different approaches to this subject, but my preference is always to try and make a cumulative case, and this is what a jigsaw guide to making sense of the world is all about.[3]

The English term *apologetics* comes from the Greek word *apologia*, which has nothing to do with saying you're sorry. The word means offering a defense or justification for a belief. Alvin Plantinga, described by *Time* magazine as one of America's leading philosophers,[4] has defended the reasonableness of Christianity by pointing out, "Perhaps the main function of apologetics is to show that . . . [we] have nothing whatsoever for which to apologize."[5] So if life has dented your confidence in the gospel, or difficult questions are an obstacle to sharing the Christian faith, a jigsaw guide brings good news: there is hope of sharing the hope that you have.

The first thing to do is always the thing to do first, so chapter one will help you learn to use the jigsaw to put life's broken pieces back together. Chapter two will give you a good grasp of truth, the cornerstone of every belief—despite incessant attacks in the popular culture, you need to know that truth is shaken but not stirred. Chapter three will help you develop a firm understanding of belief. Some say it doesn't really matter what you believe as long as you are sincere, but the fact is some beliefs are better than others. Chapter four will establish an accurate definition of faith so you can respond to those who claim that faith is keeping your eyes closed. This chapter makes clear that biblical faith is walking forward with your eyes open. Chapter five will help you recapture a healthy respect for doubt, something often denigrated as a sign of weakness. It is important to understand that doubt can be respectable, biblical and compatible with confident belief. Finally, chapter six will put the pieces together so you can know the truth, defend your belief, anchor your faith, deal with doubt and show how Christianity paints the big picture.

This book is written to encourage those who hold a Christian worldview, but it also has something important to say to those who do not see the world this way—and who seek the truth. A jigsaw guide will work whatever your worldview, and the subsequent chapters will engage non-Christians on two levels. It challenges them to think how successfully their worldview paints the big picture and puts life's broken pieces back together, and it offers a big-picture perspective on the Christian worldview so that non-Christians can understand what Christians believe and why they believe it. I should add a warning: Christianity makes a powerful case. Indeed, that's why many people would rather not crack open the Christian worldview—they're afraid they'll be drawn closer to a place they don't want to go. However, there's no need to worry. Even the best reasons to believe are never compulsory. Non-Christians will always retain the freedom to walk away. Choosing to embrace the Christian faith and follow Jesus Christ is the result of a super-natural work of God that goes much deeper. More than engaging the mind, the Holy Spirit strikes a chord in the depths of the soul and provokes humility, repentance and the faith to believe.

So if reason falls short of persuading others to accept the truth and teaching of Christianity, why is it so important to share our reasons to believe? First, God wants us to love him with our hearts, souls, bodies and minds (Mt 22:37)—with everything. We cannot dismiss our intellect without ignoring the way God created us. Second, reason is one of the ways God draws people closer to himself. While reason alone cannot bring about real change and is not designed to transform people, it is still a tool to connect and communicate the truth, one that clears away unnecessary intel-lectual obstacles. Third, the Bible clearly states that Christians are responsible to share why they believe, and both Scripture and human history record how important this can be. Some people pepper us with questions to avoid dealing with real issues, but others genuinely seek the truth and run aground on the rocks of reasons to reject Christianity—which can be overcome.

Sharing one's faith is the biblical responsibility of every Christian, but it's important to distinguish between what falls on our shoulders and what does not fall on our shoulders. Christians are not responsible to make anyone believe anything (we cannot) or to bash them over the head with the Bible until they say they do (we should not). Christians are to reflect the character of Christ and share the truth with love, gentleness and respect (1 Pet 3:15). Do this faithfully and you have not failed, even if people reject the message. It's important to respect others and allow them the right to hold and express a different view (the true definition of tolerance), and sometimes we need to agree to disagree—without being disagreeable.

Christians share because they care, and while it can be heartbreaking when people we love choose to reject this important message, it helps to remember that the end of one conversation is not necessarily the end of the story. While God can suddenly intervene in a person's life in a dramatic way, he also gently draws people closer to the truth over time. So believers need to be patient, prayerful and prepared to add another link in the chain: strengthening the greater work God is doing one conversation at a time. Sitting back and doing nothing because "the Holy Spirit will take care of it" flies in the face of biblical teaching. All Christians are responsible to do their part, do their best, and trust God to take care of the rest.

The Christian worldview resonates with people because it lines up with the way we see and experience the world in critical areas. When believers can demonstrate that their faith is reasonable, life-changing and true, God will take their words and supernaturally drive them home to greater effect. Some who hear this message will reject it and go in another direction despite our best efforts, but others will be drawn closer and make a decision to trust in Jesus Christ. These are conversations that count for eternity, so non-Christians should be willing to hear what Christians have to say, even if they decide to walk away. Christians on the other hand must be ready to have these kinds of conversations. Many struggle because they believe that engaging others is out of reach, but the jigsaw lowers the bottom rung on the ladder to confident Christianity so everyone can climb on board. Simply start where people are, work with what you know, and when you learn to put the pieces together and make sense of the world you will discover you're prepared to share—anywhere!

1

JIGSAW

Be Prepared to See It

*"Life is puzzling—the greatest puzzle of them all—
but what if you could make sense of the world?"*

"You can't because we'll never have all the answers!"

*"But like when you're doing a jigsaw, you don't need every piece
of the puzzle to see the big picture. All you need is enough
important parts that stand out and fit together."*

The ordinary jigsaw puzzle serves as a guide to making sense of the world. But if you dare to suggest this, some people may decide you have a few pieces missing. Conversations about life's toughest questions result in raised eyebrows, rolled eyes and shrugged shoulders because people know we will never have all the answers. However, you do not need every piece of a puzzle to see the big picture. All you need is enough important parts that stand out and fit together. Ultimate answers are within reach of ordinary people when you understand you do not need to know everything to know the truth, and the jigsaw encourages you to start putting the pieces together.

Imagine the wonder of waking up every morning knowing you have discovered the meaning of life—and that it is good news. What would you do? Who would you tell? It may sound too good to be true, but this should be the confident claim of every Christian. Followers of Jesus Christ hold a belief that is supernaturally signed and sealed, but it is also a faith anchored in the real world. Christian apologist Ravi Zacharias has defended this message in some of the most prestigious religious, academic and political settings around the world. He notes, "God has a script. He has spoken of it in His Scriptures. Finding the script moves us closer to solving the mystery."[1]

Life is mysterious, but God's natural revelation is designed to shine light on the truth and point us in the direction of his supernatural revelation (Rom 1:20; Ps 19:1). As author Paul Little has said, "God expects us to believe in him based on comprehensible evidence. He gives us intelligent and logical reasons. He is saying, 'Look at the natural world, even the universe or your own body and you will have ample evidence for belief.'"[2]

G. K. Chesterton is one of my favorite authors. A prolific and engaging writer, he has been described as a man of colossal genius, and his classic work *Orthodoxy* powerfully captures the role of reason in his journey to Christian faith. It also discusses the limits of responsibility when it comes to sharing one's faith with others: "It is the purpose of the writer to attempt an explanation, not of whether the Christian faith can be believed, but of how he personally has come to believe it."[3] As a Christian, I am responsible to share why I believe what I believe with those who are willing to listen. I cannot make anyone believe anything, nor should I try. Yet like Chesterton I firmly believe that ultimate answers are within the reach of everyone who is prepared to look for them with open eyes and an open mind. We will never exhaust the wonders of this world but we can still grasp—and gasp at—the significance of the big picture.

Whenever we are disillusioned by missing pieces of the puzzle or parts that don't seem to fit, we can turn our attention to things that do snap into place. There is a basic level of revelation that allows everyone to grasp something of the wonder of this world without ever exhausting the depths of knowledge available. Chesterton demonstrates this paradox powerfully: "The good news is so simple a child can understand it at once, and so subtle that the greatest intellects never quite get to the bottom of it."[4] We will never complete the puzzle of this world, but people of all ages and stages can do enough to see the big picture, and the jigsaw puzzle provides a simple mechanism that drives home this wonderful reality.

A Strategy That Comes Naturally
Earlier, in the introduction, I described how my daughter was able to look at the jumbled pieces of a Cinderella puzzle and snap them into place. But what if she was able to do this only because she had seen the box? Sophia may have switched her attention to the puzzle pieces, yet it's possible she was relying on her previous exposure to the picture to guide her. In real life we don't have this advantage; we are not granted direct access to life's big picture— which is the reason many people are so confused. And any illustration that offers hope of making sense of the real world must take this into consideration.

Jigsaw 2.0. Let's consider a situation where Sophia is confronted by a puzzle and hasn't had access to the big picture. We'll call this illustration jigsaw 2.0. Let's say there was a mix-up at the factory and the Cinderella puzzle pieces were placed in a box with a picture of Sleeping Beauty on it. Sophia is given the jigsaw, but she does not have the picture on the box to guide her. Even worse, she doesn't know she's contending with the wrong box. This would be a frustrating experience, and the disparity would encourage her to eventually forget about the box and focus entirely on the puzzle pieces. What is curious—and crucial—is we would expect her to find a way to snap important pieces into place, perhaps enough to see the big picture begin to emerge.

Still, while Sophia lacks the right picture in her hand, she still has the right picture in her mind. She's already familiar with Cinderella. Perhaps through sheer luck she stumbles on the fact that this is what the jigsaw represents. If so, her progress from that point on will still owe everything to having the right guide, albeit one planted in her mind rather than painted on a box. If this explains the outcome, then once again the illustration loses its luster. Skeptics will contend that in real life we don't have access to the big picture—one painted on a box or planted in our mind.

Jigsaw 3.0. We need to anticipate this objection and undercut it by going straight to jigsaw 3.0. This time Sophia is given a blank box with a Dinderella puzzle inside. (Dinderella is my imaginary addition to the princess hall of fame; I'm willing to develop her if Disney shows an interest.) Sophia has no previous knowledge of this character. There is no concrete image to guide her—in her mind or on a box. Yet we would still expect her to find a way to fit things together. Examining the broken puzzle would take more time, but she could still snap important pieces into place. With patience and perseverance, Sophia would do enough to start to glimpse the big picture, discovering the general nature of this new character without knowing her name or what she looks like, and this suggests that something else is going on.

Sophia has a basic level of understanding about the world— prior knowledge of the way princesses (or people) are and ought to be—and this helps her recognize particular patterns that stand out and fit together. She never really starts with a clean slate or works with a blank canvas; she has a fuzzy familiarity that allows her to look at a broken puzzle and naturally put pieces together. This admission does not undermine the jigsaw approach to making sense of the world. In fact, it provides the transition we need to illustrate why it works.

Sophia can look at a broken puzzle with a sense of the way things are and ought to be, and the jigsaw analogy suggests that we look at the world the same way. We do not start out in life with a clean slate, nor do we work with a blank canvas. We have a fuzzy familiarity with the world that helps us see that it is broken, and this allows us to put important pieces back together. There may be no concrete image in our minds to guide us, but there is a degree of awareness that makes particular pieces of the puzzle stand out and get our attention. Whether it's Cinderella, Dinderella or making sense of the world, we have a basic ability to snap a number of important things into place, and if we can do enough to see the big picture we will have good reason to believe we know the truth.[5]

A Respect for Common Sense
These basic beliefs are the reason we can naturally pick out pieces of a puzzle or identify the way things are and ought to be, and this is the basis for a jigsaw guide to making sense of the world. We enjoy a basic level of intuition sometimes referred to as common sense. Thomas Reid was a philosopher in eighteenth-century Scotland who defended and defined common sense as "those propositions that properly functioning adult human beings . . . explicitly believe or take for granted in their ordinary activities and practices."[6] No doubt the key phrase is "properly functioning"—who gets to decide that, anyway?—but the point is that Reid defended the right of ordinary people to look at life and know what is right and true.

Of course, we can be wrong about what we take to be principles of common sense and should thus be cautious, Reid emphasizes.[7] Common sense is more than just taking a vote. The changing tides of public opinion have shown that the majority is not always right, and in real terms we can never ascertain what the real majority is—or what people really believe. But if we believe something to be true, we should be able to trace our finger through the fabric of this world and find that others generally see it and believe it too. At the very least we ought to be able to make a good case that our beliefs line up with the natural order of things.

We will often encounter great debate and disagreement on this point, but our responsibility is only to anchor our beliefs on a reasonable foundation, offering good reasons to believe they are true. An appeal to common sense will need to be defended, particularly in a postmodern age where many people claim to believe that truth does not exist or that objective reality is out of reach. We will discuss this at length in chapter two.

Digging Deeper
You don't have to dig too deep to remind people that they do know some things are and ought to be, and some things ought not to be. But reason is never enough to convince those determined to resist a particular conclusion. I once spoke at a high school conference on ethical issues and one student was eager to speak to me afterward. He rejected my defense of absolute moral values, defiantly stating, "It all depends on the situation." I said I appreciated that there are gray areas when it comes to ethics, adding, "But surely we can know that particular acts—for example, the torture of innocent children for fun—are absolutely wrong." He hesitated before shaking his head. "I couldn't say it was absolutely wrong." This kind of steely determination to turn away from an objective moral value, one that slaps us in the face, was disturbing, but he was ready to do what was necessary to keep up the pretense of his moral autonomy.

The encounter reminded me of a story told by one of my philosophy professors. J. P. Moreland is Distinguished Professor of Philosophy at Talbot School of Theology, and he once had a similar dialogue with a student who was holding tight to everyone's right to do what they want. Eventually J. P. pretended to end the conversation and walk away, stopping only long enough to pick up the student's music player on his way out the door. As the young man rose to his feet in protest, J. P. paused and asked why this was a problem.[8] In practice we do not really support everyone's right to do what they want, but we like to superficially suggest it whenever it's convenient, using it as a thinly veiled warning for people to leave us alone.

Identifying examples of absolute right and absolute wrong is a powerful way to start talking about things that really matter. We can make a good case for the way the world ought to be and ought not to be. It is worth sounding a note of caution: this will take us into sensitive areas, so we need to tread carefully—but the fact is we need to tread. There is a natural order that we can recognize, standards above and beyond us that serve as an ultimate guide to putting things right. Even Greek philosopher Plato said, "In heaven . . . there is laid up a pattern for it, methinks, which he who desires may behold, and beholding, may set his own house in order."[9] So our goal should be to discern and learn from this heavenly sense of direction, snapping things into place on earth so we can see the big picture and start living in light of the truth.

The challenge is that every religion claims to grant such heavenly insight, and many peer groups will pull together to defend what is common sense, at least to them. They may even point to a few pieces of the puzzle that seem to go together and support their view. A small sample of life can give you a glimpse of the big picture but it can also distort it, and when someone has drifted off course we need to try to steer them back in the right direction. Raising questions and reflecting on critical issues encourages people to stand back and take stock, and we can share the reasons we believe our worldview fills in critical gaps and captures the big picture better than anything else. Our goal is to arrive at that "Eureka!" moment when someone starts to make sense of the world. But a number of obstacles stand in the way.

Obstacles to Putting the Theory into Practice

Obstacles to putting a jigsaw guide into practice are significant but not insurmountable. Certainly there are no easy answers to life's difficult questions (by definition), but with patience and perseverance we can do enough to see the big picture. It is worth the effort of doing what it takes to see life in its true context.

Respected author and literary critic Terry Eagleton has pointed out the challenges posed by a sedentary society addicted to passive engagement with the world. Eagleton says, "Nobody who emerges from a regular eight-hours-a-day television viewing is likely to be quite the same self-identical subject who once conquered India or annexed the Caribbean."[10] Some people will decide that grappling with life's difficult questions sounds like too much hard work, but Thomas Morris, former professor at the University of Notre Dame and founder of the Morris Institute of Human Values, firmly believes the rewards are there for those who want to make sense of it all. He says, "Not everyone has the evidential itch, but for those who do, the means for scratching it is available."[11]

For those still concerned about the difficulty of the road that lies ahead, I encourage you to read on and remember that even the longest journey is shorter after the first step. Do not let others dissuade you or discourage you. In the face of opposition feel free to quote this powerful proverb with a smile: "The man (or woman) who says it cannot be done shouldn't interrupt the man (or woman) who is doing it."

The First Obstacle: A Random World

If you were presented with a completely random assortment of broken puzzle pieces, there would be no point trying to fit things together. You could amuse yourself by creating pretty patterns, but there would be nothing reasonable or rational for you to discover. The first obstacle relates to the fact that some people look at the world the same way and come to the same conclusion. Influential atheist philosopher Bertrand Russell won the Nobel Prize for literature in 1950, and he famously said we are simply "the accidental outcome of a collocation of atoms."[12] If this is true, the world is only a random collection of broken parts that will not make sense in any satisfying way, and it's not worth the effort to look for ultimate answers when the world is the result of cosmic disorder.

But it's worth considering how an accidental outcome of a collocation of atoms is able to figure out that he is an accidental outcome of a collocation of atoms. As John Gray has argued, "If Darwin's theory of natural selection is true . . . the human mind serves evolutionary success, not truth,"[13] and the outworking of atheism is that "humans cannot be other than irrational. Curiously, this is a conclusion that few rationalists have been ready to accept."[14] Gray has written several books on politics and philosophy, and his honesty about the logical consequences of atheism is admirable, particularly since he seems to hold an atheistic outlook on life.[15] One cannot help but wonder about the self-defeating nature of Russell's statement. Chesterton remarked on this kind of curiosity (with a smile, I am sure): "Descartes said, 'I think; therefore I am!' The philosophic evolutionist reverses and negates this epigram. He says, 'I am not; therefore I cannot think.'"[16] However, let us be gracious and give Russell (and Gray?) the benefit of the doubt, thinking for a moment about this natural perspective, since it drives the anchor of the first obstacle deep into the ground.

Without God's glasses. Seeing the world without God's glasses means seeing reality as a random array of broken bits and pieces and, as a consequence, our lives as insignificant pieces of a meaningless puzzle. This worldview has special prominence in our culture. Indeed, it shapes many people's outlook on life, and if it's true, we are simply the byproduct of a cosmic accident. I enjoy standing up in schools and being open and honest about what this means for young people today: You are a grown-up germ! What surprises me is that a secular education that preaches this with such passion wrinkles its collective forehead when students take it to heart and start acting like it. We rebuke rowdy students for behaving like animals—after indoctrinating them with the belief that they are animals. What should we expect from an evolved bacterium that has learned to survive by selfishly promoting its own ends and eradicating everything that stands in its way?

Despite this embarrassing ancestry, atheists still like to inject meaning into a meaningless existence, as the *Philosopher's Magazine* cofounder Julian Baggini demonstrates: "What most atheists do believe is that although there is only one kind of stuff in the universe and it is physical, out of this stuff comes minds, beauty, emotions, moral values—in short the full gamut of phenomena that gives richness to human life."[17] A natural ability to recognize this world of wonders comes as no surprise to those who hold a Christian worldview, but the real issue is that a godless perspective has no philosophical justification for it. In other words, Baggini et al. are writing existential checks their worldview cannot cash.

The culture continues to promote this general outlook on life, albeit indirectly, by bowing to the so-called hard sciences, although many people are unaware of it. I spoke on this subject at a special event, highlighting the way public schools are reinforcing a godless worldview. A few Christian teachers came to speak to me afterward, slightly annoyed. They pointed to the significant input and influence of Christian organizations and individual teachers, but they failed to see the way religion in general (and Christianity in particular) has been marginalized and compartmentalized in public education. Naturalism is the driving force, depicting a world where "everything is composed of natural entities—those studied by the sciences."[18] While naturalism is not identical to physicalism (the belief the world is only composed of physical things), the two are united in rejecting the supernatural. According to naturalism, a supernatural perspective may be permitted, even promoted as a source of comfort to those who need to lean on it or are curious about it, but the hard facts come from the hard sciences and they absolutely deny anything else.[19]

It is naive to think the classroom can ever be unbiased or philosophically neutral. A worldview is woven into every curriculum. I was invited to debate the director of education for the British Humanist Association on national radio in the U.K., responding to the question "Should schools teach creationism?" I said I had no problem with schools presenting an antisupernatural philosophy in the science classroom. For example, stating that the universe came into existence from nothing is a philosophical statement, not a scientific fact. (Note: this statement actually contradicts everything we know and learn from using the scientific method.) However, my contention was that whenever this position was presented the students deserved to hear the counterperspective: a supernatural explanation that would redress the philosophical balance (and present a more rational basis for belief).

When it comes to addressing life's big questions, we need to defend the right to speak and hear the evidence from all sides, and the Christian worldview stands in direct opposition to any godless outlook on life. Atheism is the overt belief that "God does not exist," but it generally squares with naturalism, so I will refer to both positions throughout this book to point out the weaknesses of a worldview without God. Some people who hold this worldview already know there is a lack of ammunition for atheism, so they claim a softer or negative version, saying they merely lack good reasons to believe God exists. The attraction is obvious: You are free to criticize theism without having to defend atheism. But William Lane Craig unmasks this maneuver. Craig has successfully debated atheists in some of the world's most prestigious universities, and he says this kind of "atheism ceases to be a view. . . . On this redefinition, even babies, who hold no opinion at all on the matter, count as atheists! In fact, our cat Muff counts as an atheist on this definition, since she has (to my knowledge) no belief in God."[20]

The union of naturalism and atheism seems like a marriage made in heaven, but when you appreciate how these worldviews work together there is no honeymoon on the horizon. Why? Life is futile! This would seem like grounds for divorce, but there is no escape. Ultimate futility is simply a harsh reality we need to deal with, and we will be doing the next generation a favor by helping them to grow up and grasp the nettle. If I believed this worldview were true there would be no point writing this book (or any book) to encourage people to look for ultimate answers.

Some would argue this is an overreaction: We should take a more humble approach, pointing our pen in the direction of things that breathe meaning and purpose into our lives. The trouble is that beliefs have consequences, and we cannot have it both ways. A worldview without God means that any subjective sense of meaning is only papering over the cracks of ultimate futility, and any recognition of a deeper sense of meaning in the world requires the existence of something above and beyond us. So when people appreciate that there are things of value in this world—and their worldview does not measure up—we need to carefully bring this to their attention.

The importance of an open discussion. In order to find the truth we need to be prepared to talk about things that really matter, and Christians should never deny atheists the right to have their say. This is crucial in the public square, although the imbalance currently swings in the other direction. Many atheists who claim to support "free thinking" are responsible for suppressing free thought—silencing those who disagree with them.[21] I always find this surprising, particularly when atheists claim Christianity is weak and represents a worldview found wanting. In a debate you do not deny vulnerable opponents the right to speak; you gladly bring them out into the open, place the microphone in their hand, and encourage the audience to be quiet and pay attention. A weak opponent will place the noose around his own neck.

I am thrilled when people have an opportunity to hear what atheism has to say, particularly when Christians can stand on the same platform and point out the logical consequences of this worldview. Atheism results in a world where there is no basis for rationality, human beings have no intrinsic value, life has no absolute meaning, and there is no hope for the future—all beliefs that strike us as deeply problematic. It is not just that these conclusions are uncomfortable; they completely contradict our experience and fall short of our expectations.

The idea that the world is meaningless does not sit comfortably with us, and this should raise a red flag. To suggest that we are simply an insignificant part of a meaningless picture troubles us and reveals something very important. We do not live like this is true, we do not want to live like this is true, and we are unable to live like this is true. So it is worth considering why we should believe this is true when we seem to be wired for so much more. Turn your attention for a moment to the Christian worldview and you discover there is a basis for rationality, every person has absolute value, life has real meaning, and there is hope for the future. When you discover that a number of important arrows are pointing in one direction, it makes sense to pay attention. Atheism, on the other hand, seems to be pointing us in the wrong direction. We need to engage those whose minds have been subtly saturated by this way of thinking to share the reasons it does not fit and is not true. Christians are called to invest their hearts, minds and souls in meeting this challenge, and when we share the good news it is tremendously exciting to see eternal hope rise from the ashes of ultimate despair.

G. K. Chesterton and C. S. Lewis unmask the insufficiency of a godless worldview grounded in meaninglessness, pointing out, "Christian optimism is based on the fact that we do not fit this world,"[22] and "If I find in myself a desire which no experience in this world can satisfy, the most probable explanation is that I was made for another world."[23] We are born with the expectation that the world ought to make sense, life really means something, and we live in hope of finding ultimate answers. Naturalism, curiously enough, does not come naturally, and despite the pressure of a secular society that indirectly promotes these "values," our internal compass stubbornly steers us in another direction. This overcomes the suggestion that there is no point in trying to make sense of the world—there is—or that we have no hope of finding ultimate answers—we do. So we are ready to move on and consider the next obstacle to a jigsaw guide to making sense of the world: what about the picture on the box?

The Second Obstacle: A World Without a Box
Typically, a jigsaw puzzle arrives with a picture on the box that represents the goal and also acts as a guide to solving the problem. Unfortunately, many people believe that real life does not come with a picture on the box, at least not one everyone agrees on. So how do you begin a journey when you don't know where you're going or how you'll get there? There is a story about a man who was hopelessly lost and asked for directions only to hear, "Well, if I were you, I wouldn't start from here." When it comes to making sense of the world many feel a similar sentiment, but there is a way to break this vicious circle and move forward.

There are generally two ways to tackle a jigsaw puzzle: top-down and bottom-up. The top-down method is when you start with a big picture and search for puzzle pieces that correspond to it. The bottom-up approach is when you immediately start trying to snap the puzzle pieces into place. Typically you employ both methods at the same time, but when it comes to solving the puzzle of the world we will consider each in turn. The top-down approach overcomes the second obstacle (a world without a box), and we will return to the bottom-up approach when we focus on the third obstacle (a world of broken pieces).

A top-down approach. The beauty of the top-down approach is that it addresses the concerns of someone who looks at life and wonders how to find the right guide to making sense of the world. Many people assume we live in a world without the box, yet many others are looking for the right box to fit this world. Look around and you see that there is no lack of ultimate guides on offer, but how do you know which one is the right one—if any of them are? The best way to begin is to choose one and put it to the test. Every worldview claims to paint the big picture, representing the right way to see the real world; therefore it should connect with life's broken pieces. The more it corresponds to critical things that stand out in this world, the more we will be inclined to believe it is accurate—and truly reflects the big picture. So when you hear someone say we cannot make sense of the world because we cannot be sure we have the right guide, ask them: why not try one to see how it measures up?

All individuals have a worldview, whether or not they realize it, and it's possible to put your worldview to the test to see what it's made of. No one can boast of twenty-twenty vision when it comes to making sense of the world, but we can discover the extent of our shortsightedness. Francis Schaeffer was a Christian author and speaker who was responsible for starting L'Abri Fellowship, a community that has grown into an international network of study centers for those seeking answers to life's ultimate questions. He noted, "People's presuppositions lay a grid for all they bring forth into the external world. Their presuppositions also provide a basis for their values and therefore the basis for their decisions. 'As a man thinketh, so is he.'"[24] Internal forces are at work that taint the way we see things, so we do not approach the world directly as a blank slate, or *tabula rasa*,[25] but neither do we have the power to "create a world or environment from scratch and then live in it," says R. C. Sproul. "Rather we step into a world and culture that already exists, and we learn to interact with it."[26] There is an objective world out there, existing in spite of us and independent from us. And while some things are out of focus and out of reach, there are times when we can directly engage with the world and see it as it is.

Does it measure up? We all have a worldview, but this does not mean we are locked in to a particular perspective. Any disconnect between what we expect and what we experience will raise the question: does my worldview really measure up? Some people may choose to ignore or deny any irregularities, but when our goal is to know the truth, we will keep moving in its direction. Christians have good reasons to believe the Christian worldview does measure up and helps us make the best sense of the world, and the critical weaknesses of a godless perspective only strengthen this conviction. Naturalism generally reflects Greek philosopher Protagoras's famous quip that man is the measure of all things, since human beings seem to be the only ones doing any measuring, but when we take this seriously it sends us on a downward spiral. As Schaeffer eloquently states, "Man beginning with his proud, proud humanism, tried to make himself autonomous, but rather than becoming great, he had found himself ending up as only a collection of molecules."[27]

Earlier I pointed out the hollow outcome of viewing the human race as a byproduct of a chemical collision, and some people even suggest that it more closely resembles a virus. "The human species is now so numerous as to constitute a serious planetary malady . . . a plague of people."[28] If this big picture is true, our lives do not add up to much. Those who hold to naturalism do not shout this from the rooftops but it is the logical outworking of their worldview. It presents the picture on the box and suggests that it is up to us (or others) whether to assign value to human existence. We should be thankful that most atheists who hold this view do not practice what they preach.

Those with the power to promote this kind of godless ideology have demonstrated how damaging it can be. The pages of human history were deeply stained when Hitler attached his political ambition to a philosophy inspired by the writings of atheist philosopher Friedrich Nietzsche. Nietzsche preached Darwin's survival of the fittest, arguing that our creed should be to ensure the evolution of human beings and the realization of their full potential through the "will to power."[29] Hitler embraced this ideology and put it into practice, combining it with his Darwinian ideals focused on survival of the strong.[30] When people talk about survival of the fittest, they tend to forget the other side of the coin: eradication of the weak.[31] Hitler did not, and six million people lost their lives when they were deemed worse than worthless and weeded out of the human gene pool.

Many of Darwin's defenders argue that any social application of his theories is a misapplication, but on what basis? How can you defend the red tooth and claw of the animal kingdom and then suggest that it does not apply to us? Peter Singer is an ethicist from Princeton University who would argue that this is simply speciesism: "a prejudice or attitude of bias toward the interests of members of one's own species and against those of members of another species."[32] Naturalism is a worldview that runs into trouble when we try to use it consistently as a guide to life, and our persistent belief in human life as absolutely valuable is a serious stumbling block to its success. It presents the kind of big picture that does not make sense of the world, others or ourselves, and this is a good reason to reject it and look for another to take its place.

The Christian worldview presents a radically different top-down approach. Rather than undermine the belief that human life is absolutely valuable, the biblical perspective promotes it and provides a reasonable basis for it. Every human being is made by God, for God and in the image of God. This means every person is stamped with absolute value, and it is not up to us to assign value to human beings or take it away. This cornerstone of Christian belief has motivated acts of kindness and sacrifice throughout history. Jesus himself set the ultimate standard of altruism by giving everything—literally—for everyone else. This is the kind of behavior that is generally lauded and applauded, deemed to be a good thing, even described as something we ought to do—but why? A popular cosmetics company coined a phrase that inadvertently answers this question and captures the ethos of the Christian worldview: "Because you're worth it!"

Some people may argue that the Christian worldview merely gets lucky on this particular issue, so we need to consider more pieces of the puzzle to see if they fit quite so snugly (and we will). Yet there is no doubt that on this particular issue the Christian worldview is vastly superior. Other people might claim that I am cherry-picking beliefs that endorse a Christian perspective; however, I am not embarrassed at honing in on this particular cherry. The value of human life, in real terms, is one of the most fundamental issues we can address, and to dismiss the fact that Christianity explains it and sustains it is like cutting off your nose to spite your face. We cannot deny that there are difficult pieces of the puzzle, whatever our worldview, but the jigsaw encourages us to build on the things that do make sense and do the best we can fitting the other pieces together. If we have enough pieces in place, we can be confident we know the truth.

Some Christians are uncomfortable with the idea of putting the Christian worldview to the test, and it can be a daunting prospect when you are not really sure if you can explain the reasons you believe it to be true. However, some go further and altogether reject the idea that you need to prove anything when it comes to God: you shall not put God to the test (Mt 4:7; Deut 6:16)! Clearly, testing God is something we should not do, but here we are only evaluating a godly perspective—not God himself. The Bible encourages this kind of "taste and see" approach to discovering the truth (Ps 34:8; 1 Thess 5:21), and any worldview worth its salt will not be afraid of the top-down challenge. It would be refreshing to see more advocates of naturalism employ it, too, to see how their worldview measures up.[33]

The Third Obstacle: A World of Broken Pieces
We now turn our attention to the third obstacle, switching to a bottom-up approach to making sense of the world. Instead of starting with the picture on the box that represents a particular worldview, we focus directly on the broken pieces of life to see whether anything stands out and gets our attention.

The bottom-up approach. Just as you can look at an ordinary puzzle and pick out corners, straight edges, and colorful details, so we can naturally identify things in the real world that help us understand more about life and see it in its true context. This chapter has already considered the belief that human beings are absolutely valuable, working from the top down, and we seem to know this is true from the bottom up, without referring to a big picture. There is something special about a person that sets him or her apart from other physical things, and our natural ability to recognize this helps us build a worldview that resembles reality.

Another important piece of the puzzle that stands out and shapes our understanding relates to the world and where it came from. Consider the origin of the universe. There is good reason to believe the universe started to exist, and if it did, then the universe must have a cause.[34] The universe could not have brought itself into existence, since it was not around at the time, so we need to posit the existence of something outside the universe, to be responsible. While this sounds reasonable, it is often viewed as fighting talk among those who have closed their minds to such a possibility.

When you hear the statement "the universe came into existence from nothing," you cannot assume that truly means nothing. I encountered serious equivocation on this issue in a debate at the National Law Library of Scotland. Pointing out the problem with a universe that came into existence from nothing without a cause, one of my opponents, a physics teacher, accused me of ignorance: "You don't understand what nothing is. If you know a bit of physics,

nothing is not nothing, it's things emerging in and out of existence."[35] I could counter that absence of evidence is not the same as
evidence of absence. The belief that things can "emerge in and out
of existence" moves beyond the test tube, since we have no physical
apparatus to confirm something is out of existence, and if you
mean what you say it is always better to say what you mean.

Yet many people, some physicists included, will do anything to
resist the conclusion that something exists outside the physical
universe. Equivocation is employed to balance the scientific evidence that suggests the universe started from nothing with a philosophical presupposition that nothing can exist outside the
physical universe—to start it. In other words, you can talk about
a big bang while refusing to concede there had to be a big banger.
The statement "the universe started from nothing" must be subtly
manipulated in light of the profound consequences. Otherwise
you are effectively admitting something (or someone) incredibly
powerful (and personal) was responsible. As Stephen Hawking,
one of the world's giants of science, has admitted, "Many people
do not like the idea that time has a beginning, probably because it
smacks of divine intervention."[36]

Working from the bottom up, we know that human life is absolutely valuable, a universe that began to exist must have a cause,
and particular human actions and attitudes seem to be right, that
is, consider the belief that we ought to have a basic level of respect
for other people. This moral value has not always been promoted,
but wherever it has gone wrong it has resulted in serious damage
until powerful forces emerged to try to put it right. It seems to be
the way things ought to be. Philosophers may debate the merits of
objective morality, but I take comfort from the fact that those who
deny it continue to demonstrate it. Michel Foucault was a twentieth-
century French philosopher, one of the leading lights in a
movement to break free from absolute moral values, yet he could
not restrain himself in reacting to the immorality of France's war

in Algeria.[37] This brought him into conflict with others who shared his worldview, as they knew he was undermining his own position by indirectly suggesting we can make sense of the world and recognize the way things ought to be.

As you start putting the pieces together to make sense of this broken world, the first thing to do is always the thing to do first: start with what you do know. I was granted the opportunity to do this at the Scottish Parliament, and my confidence was not based on the belief that I know it all (I do not know it all, and I know that I don't). I was prepared to share because I knew I could put the pieces together and make a cumulative case for the truth and reasonableness of the Christian worldview. There remain many, many things that I do not know, but what I do know clearly stands out.

Consider the universe—where did it come from? I believe in God because something from someone is more probable than something from nothing.

Consider Jesus of Nazareth—a man who lived in a remote place with little money, no political power and no military might. He never wrote a book, taught for only three years and yet turned the history of the world upside-down. I believe that the life, teaching and impact of Jesus Christ confirms he is the Son of God.

Consider our experience—a desire for significance in a universe where we are less than a speck, a desire for relationship in a world that is socially broken and fragmented, and a desire for permanence in a life that is fleeting. I believe the Bible makes sense when it says we were made by God (significance), we were created to know God (relationship) and God wants us to spend eternity with him (permanence). As G. K. Chesterton said, the fact that we do not fit this world is the best evidence that we were made for another world, and Christianity offers the reason why.

It's fascinating that in such a diverse and complex world we share an amazing level of agreement about the way the world is and ought to be. Not that we agree on everything or automatically rubber-stamp whatever appears to be the consensus. Consensus (or what we believe the consensus to be) can often take us in the wrong direction. However, particular beliefs persist and seem to have a transcendent quality; they deserve our special attention. For example, those who experience the bitter taste of injustice feel a searing pain that suggests something significant: the reversal of a universal standard. As Chesterton observed, "Reason and justice grip the remotest and the loneliest star. . . . On plains of opal, under cliffs cut out of pearl, you would still find a notice-board, 'Thou shall not steal!'"[38] C. S. Lewis extended this thought when he remarked, "Think of a country where people were admired for running away in battle, or where a man felt proud of double-crossing all the people who had been kindest to him. You might just as well try to imagine a country where two and two made five."[39] In cases where such "universal" standards break down, we generally believe these counter-cultures to be the result of a broken understanding, and this is reinforced when those who hold such views are willing to reject them in favor of embracing another way of looking at the world.[40]

A note of caution. As Thomas Reid reminded us, this common-sense approach to putting life's broken pieces back together will always have an element of danger. Some will reject our values as uncommon, and others will adopt different values to suit their own desires. However, we need to balance those who confuse or abuse what makes sense with those who put it to good use at the other end of the moral spectrum. There are numerous examples of deeply held beliefs about the way the world ought to be that persist and break through. William Wilberforce is a good example. His life is still celebrated because of the part he played in the successful fight against slavery, and while he started out as a lonely voice in the British Parliament—he did not reflect the consensus—eventually the tide turned and truth prevailed.[41]

We can look back on two events in human history, the attempted extermination of Jewish people and the emancipation of

British slaves, and know what to remember with shame and what to remember with celebration. The fight against slavery was fought on the basis that slavery is always wrong. Wilberforce's Christian worldview gave him the basis—and impetus—to fight slavery. This resonated with people then and still strikes a chord today (with Christians and non-Christians alike) because slavery seems to reflect the way the world ought not to be.

The Fourth Obstacle: A World Out of Reach

If we pick out important pieces of the puzzle during a conversation, we should naturally find we can build momentum. One question leads to another and before we know it we are starting to fit things together. However, some conversations grind to a halt when we reveal that the goal is to try and make sense of the world. This can be enough to blow a person's mind, and I saw the fuse go one day. Sheryl and I were living in Scotland at the time, preparing to sell our house, when a man came to inspect the property with a view to providing a valuation. As we walked around I struck up a conversation, and when he asked me about my work I told him, "I work for an organization that deals with life's big questions, encouraging people to try and make sense of the world." As the last words spilled from my lips there was an instant change in his expression. He rolled his eyes and gasped, "Oh, God!" Interestingly, this is one of the conclusions many people draw when they start putting the pieces together, although I appreciate that he did not mean this in the same way. His point? Surely your time would be better spent doing something else—anything else!

Think big by starting small. We can empathize with those who think making sense of the world is a pointless exercise. The scale of the problem can be overwhelming, and that's why some people choose to stand back and hold their head in their hands. When we don't know what to do, sometimes it's easier to do nothing. However, a jigsaw guide helps us overcome the fourth obstacle,

grasping a world that seems out of reach. The answer? Think big
by starting small. Do not be daunted; just look for the next piece
of the puzzle. Take hold of what stands out in this world and then
consider what comes next.

There's a good illustration of this in the movie *What About Bob?*
The main character, played by Bill Murray, suffers from numerous
phobias and visits a respected psychiatrist who helps him move
toward recovery by introducing him to his latest book, *Baby Steps.*
Suddenly all of Bob's greatest fears are reduced to bite-sized chunks,
small enough to swallow, and he's able to move forward and overcome
them (here's the comic twist) by breaking everything down into
baby steps. When Bob leaves the psychiatrist's office he doesn't know
how he'll get home, but he's willing to put one foot in front of the
other, which is enough to get him where he needs to go. If we are
going to make sense of the world we need to take it one step at a time.
Think big by starting small, and put the pieces in place one at a time.

What does this look like? Take one important piece we've already identified: a universe that started to exist needs a cause. This
raises the next question, or presents the next piece of the puzzle:
what kind of cause? The universe that exists is incredibly ordered
and complex, which makes it hard to believe that it's the result of
unguided forces.[42] While it is possible that such a finely tuned universe is the accidental outcome of a cosmic explosion, science—as
well as our own experience—tells us that order does not tend to
come from disorder.[43] Therefore, it is more reasonable to believe
that some kind of intelligence is responsible, so we can fit these
two things together and get a better idea about the big picture: our
universe was created by an intelligence that is out of this world.

In recent years there has been a lot of publicity surrounding
prominent atheists who are dedicated to promoting a godless outlook
on life,[44] yet the belief that (some kind of) God exists is still the overwhelming default position of people in the world today. Even among
the more secular parts of the globe it is common to hear people

hedge their bets when it comes to belief in God. Why? Something about it makes sense. It is not an easy issue and raises all manner of questions, but the wonder of the world keeps steering people back in this direction. Looking through a telescope at the finely tuned universe makes it reasonable to believe that an intelligent agent is responsible. Looking through a microscope at the information programmed into the building blocks of life, which resembles the software of a computer programmer who is literally out of this world, it is reasonable to assume that someone had to be responsible.

I remember meeting a medical doctor who surprised me when he said, "Hemoglobin encouraged me to believe in God." The function of this protein in our blood shouted purpose and design, loud enough to get his attention. Even among those who eventually go a different direction, many are willing to admit that the evidence initially supports this conclusion.[45] Much in this world strongly suggests that an intelligent agent is necessary to make sense of it all, and with every piece that fits together there is more reason to believe it is true.

Undeniable truth. It is exciting when you use a jigsaw guide to making sense of the world and start to see things taking shape, and I enjoy turning to popular atheist Richard Dawkins to reinforce the way things seem to fit together. A scientist with a gift for communicating with the general public, Dawkins seems to have taken on responsibility for shooting down the reasonable foundation for all religious belief. Yet even in his book *The God Delusion* he cannot deny the remarkable truth that the planet earth resides in "the Goldilocks zone." In the story of Goldilocks and the three bears, the little girl wanders into the forest and ends up in the home of three bears. She decides to sample the three bowls of porridge on the table. The first bowl is too hot, the second too cold, so she turns to the last bowl and exclaims it is just right! This picture of perfection has been used to describe the earth's position in relation to the sun, since "it is not too hot and not too cold, but just right."[46] Hence the Goldilocks zone. The science behind this is incredibly complex, and while Dawkins and others try to put it down to unbelievable good fortune on our part,[47] the probability of this naturally occurring—as the product of unguided forces—is off the chart.[48]

For a scientist who should always make an inference to the best explanation, Dawkins seems determined to believe in anything but God. But for those who are more open-minded there should be a growing sense that something else is going on: someone or something out there must be responsible for it all. The Goldilocks zone is a great piece of this broken world that stands out and gets our attention.

Moriah, my youngest daughter, grasped this when she was four years old. She came home from nursery one day and told me a boy in her class did not believe in God. She was clearly worried about him, so I reminded her that people had different ideas about God— and that was okay. Then I encouraged her to think about why we should believe in God, and the Goldilocks zone provided a good reason to believe and a good reason to share.

This kind of revelation stirs a sense of excitement in my soul. People are not condemned to look at the stars and wonder, "Is anybody out there?" We can make sense of the world and begin to see things clearly. There are good reasons to believe that life and intelligence *out there* are responsible for what we see *down here*. Do not look at the world and be overwhelmed by the scale of the problem. Take baby steps toward finding the solution. Think big by starting small.

Conversations that count. I have used a jigsaw guide to making sense of the world in countless conversations, and many have occurred while I was sitting on a plane. This is one place we're guaranteed a captive audience, so we need to be careful not to abuse such a privileged position. Some people would rather sleep, read or plug in to an electronic contraption, but others are open to the kind of conversation they would sidestep on the ground. Perhaps this is influenced by the uncertainty that comes from dangling your feet thirty thousand feet in the air. A plane can provide a wonderful opportunity to talk about things that really matter. Flying from L.A. to Denver, I was able to talk to a young woman sitting next to me, and together we picked out a number of important pieces of life's puzzle. I established that there are good reasons to believe that God exists and that he is incredibly powerful and creative, so we turned to questions about who God is and how he relates to us. If God is responsible for this world, we should be able to look around and learn more about him. Every artist leaves his or her mark in one way or another, and we can look for God's signature in this world. Those who sniff and suggest that trying to find God is like trying to find the invisible man forget one thing: even the invisible man leaves footprints.

I asked this woman to imagine that she lived in a house with two neighbors, one on each side, with each neighbor owning a dog. She has never met or spoken to the neighbors but she looks over one fence and sees the dog lying there, alone and completely exposed. There is no shelter, no water to drink and no food to eat. All she can see is an old rag to chew on, which the dog probably found by scratching around. She does not need to meet this neighbor to know one thing: he does not care about his dog. The environment he has created tells you more than enough. However, she looks over the other fence and sees a completely different scenario. This dog has a little house, freshly painted, and inside there is food, fresh water and a warm blanket. There is even an assortment of toys to play with. My seatmate would be in no doubt that this person truly cares for his animal. The environment we create for another being, whether dog or person, suggests whether or not we really care, and switching our attention back to the real world, we can consider whether the God who created it all cares about us.

The world is no perfect place, but there are many things that are good about this world that did not have to be that way. I turned again to my new friend and asked if this planet naturally provides anything we need, to the extent we literally could not live without it. She did not take long to recognize our need for oxygen, and I reminded her of the incredible recycling process that takes place on this planet. Plants make good use of the air we breathe out so it does not go to waste, but they also function as a clean and efficient recycling system, producing oxygen we need to breathe. It's amazing to think that this is part of the natural order of things.

Then we turned our attention to water. Water that finds its way into the ocean ends up a salty substance we cannot drink, but it heats up, evaporates, cools, condenses and returns to us as fresh water; one of our greatest needs literally falls from the sky. We also talked about our basic need for food and how this planet provides a nourishing diet that comes in a colorful variety of flavors. Long ago we should have consumed everything on this planet worth eating, and we would have were it not for the fact that the parts we throw away fall into the ground and produce more—more than we started with.

However, every suggestion that the world was designed for us can be countered with an objection, some people say—that we evolved to fit the world. No doubt there is a degree of biological variation that takes place, a level of adaptability that allows living things to survive and flourish, but we are talking about an amazing degree of ongoing stability and provision. The belief that we naturally emerged, adapted to our surroundings, became conscious of our survival and managed to reproduce is hard enough to swallow, but to add the level of constant planetary care and concern seems to push the limits of credulity. Instead, we fit these things together and build momentum toward the belief that an all-powerful God is responsible, demonstrating creativity and intelligence that are out of this world, and this God has shown deep concern for us by providing the essential things we need. As each piece of the puzzle fits together we grow in confidence that each piece is the right piece, and while there will always be pieces that do not seem to fit or parts that are missing, we can build on the things we do know until we know enough to know the truth.

The Fifth and Final Obstacle: A World That Is Not Enough

A jigsaw guide to making sense of the world encourages us to pick out important pieces of the puzzle and start fitting things together, but when it comes to seeing the big picture the question remains: how much is enough? When I teach on this subject I often show an image of the *Mona Lisa* loosely reflected on the broken pieces of a jigsaw. The puzzle is not complete, many pieces are still missing, but a number of important parts are in place. When I ask the class to identify the picture, generally everyone raises his or her hand. I like to feign hesitation and argue that there are still pieces to be found, but this does not deter anyone because they know enough to know the truth.

If on another occasion I showed a smaller number of pieces revealing the image, some might decide to be more cautious; however, you can be sure that others would still believe they could see the big picture. It would be no surprise for one person to say, "I can see the big picture!" and another to say, "I need more pieces in place!" While the more pieces you have the better, in the end it's up to the individual to decide when enough is enough to know the truth.

When it comes to making sense of the world, it's not all about snapping things into place. There are crucial differences between seeing the *Mona Lisa* and grasping the meaning of life. The former has nothing to say about how you live your life, but the latter threatens to turn your world upside-down. So when you're helping someone put the pieces together, you need to be aware of other barriers that stand in the way.

Other Barriers

Christianity is entirely reasonable and we need to share good reasons to believe it, but making the intellectual case clears away only one level of obstacles. There are still reasons to reject the big picture, and among the most powerful are moral, emotional and spiritual reasons.

Moral resistance. Josh McDowell is one of the most recognized and respected Christian speakers in the world today. He wrote the bestseller *Evidence That Demands a Verdict*, which became a landmark in modern Christian apologetics. As a young man McDowell rigorously investigated the Christian faith with the purpose of disproving Christianity, but as the pieces snapped into place he found himself starting to believe it was true. Yet he was still reluctant to take the next step:

> You would think that after examining the evidence, I would have immediately jumped on board and become a Christian. But in spite of the abundant evidence, I felt a strong reluctance to make the plunge. My mind was convinced of the truth. I had to admit that Jesus Christ must be exactly who he claimed to be. I could plainly see that Christianity was not a myth, not a fantasy of wishful dreamers, not a hoax played on the simple-minded, but rock-solid truth. I knew the truth, yet my will was pulling me in another direction. There were two reasons for my reluctance: pleasure and pride.[49]

Multiple barriers stand in the way of someone hearing, understanding and embracing the Christian worldview. So when it comes to knowing how much is enough to see the big picture, Christians are responsible only to prayerfully and practically do their best and trust God to take care of the rest. We need to live as a good example of the truth, speak in a way that makes people think about the truth, and allow God to deal with the heart of the matter—the matter of the heart.[50]

Jesus understood this better than anyone, and he exposed the underlying obstacles in his conversation with a rich young ruler (Mt 19:16-22). This man appeared to be ready to follow Jesus, having overcome the intellectual obstacles and realizing he spoke the truth; however, his instructions to "go sell your possessions and give to the poor" identified the greater issue and the real stumbling block. Instead of doing what Jesus asked, the man turned and walked away. You do not have to be rich to count the cost of following Christ because we all understand the aversion to giving up what we cling to in life. God requires us to let go and let him take control, while we are determined to hang on to our life with white knuckles. Moral obstacles are often what really stand in the way of people embracing the truth of the Christian worldview, and when this is the case no reason to believe will ever be good enough.

Hitting back in hurt. Emotions are another powerful force at work in our lives, and when we have been deeply wounded in some way it is not unusual to take this out on God. I have read the arguments of some of Christianity's fiercest critics, and what they lack in substance they generally make up for with rage or sarcasm. A degree of knowledge about God can encourage this response, because God has revealed that he chooses to make himself vulnerable to our actions and attitudes; people can cause God pain (Gen 6:6; Eph 4:30). Among those who resist him the most are those trying to hurt him the best. C. S. Lewis was reflecting on his own experience when he said, "All that stuff about the cosmic sadist was not so much the expression of thought as of hatred. I was getting from it the only pleasure a man in anguish can get; the pleasure of hitting back."[51]

Other people may be less vindictive but equally scarred by life's circumstances. They would rather resist God if it means they can hold on to their pain or anger. Christianity offers forgiveness from God, but it also demands that we be willing to forgive others (and ourselves). When the greater attraction is holding a grudge against those responsible for our deepest hurts, emotional barriers will stand between us and doing what it takes to embrace the Christian worldview.

Spiritual blindness. Another obstacle that leads to resistance, perhaps starting out as a moral or emotional barrier, is spiritual blindness. The Bible says everyone has a natural inclination to resist God's truth and revelation in the world (Jn 3:19-20), so you could say we are all spiritually shortsighted. No one can see the truth until God supernaturally makes the truth known. However, some people persist in denying God's revelation (and prompting) for so long that their hearts become hardened (Ps 95:8; Heb 3:8). This is not irrevocable, since God will open eyes and reveal the truth to all those who genuinely seek it (Jer 29:12-13), but when spiritual blindness stands in the way there is nothing more you can do or say but pray.

When I was a student at seminary I found a part-time job gardening for a retired couple, and while the lady was very warm and friendly to me her husband had a strong revulsion toward Christianity. It was intense in a way I had never witnessed before. I could not even raise the subject of my studies without him hardening his expression and turning away, as if something seized him from within. There was no willingness to discuss anything related to the Christian worldview, and he made me think of a seafarer determined to remain onboard as captain of his ship even when that ship was sinking. The tragedy was that this man wasn't in good health, and in real terms his ship was sinking, but he seemed determined to grit his teeth and resist anything I could do or say.

While I look back on this I regret never breaking through this barrier to talk about things that really matter, but I take heart from the fact that no one is out of reach of the truth. In fact, the apostle Paul, one of the greatest ambassadors of the Christian message, started out as one of its fiercest opponents. A violent persecutor of Christians, he was determined to eradicate Christian faith from the world, and there is no natural explanation for why his life completely turned around. That is why Paul's conversion has been long regarded as a substantial evidence for the truth of

Christianity.[52] I can only hope that the power of God was at work in this man's life too, able to turn things around in time.

The best worldview is always the one that resonates with reality. While some people automatically rule out anything supernatural, there is no valid reason to do so—without demonstrating an antisupernatural bias. We should be open to natural and supernatural explanations as we try to make sense of the world, and the Christian worldview draws from both realms to put the pieces together. Seeing the big picture is never enough for someone to embrace Christianity and follow Jesus Christ; however, demonstrating that it is the best way to make sense of the world will do three important things: those who grasp it will have reason to hold on to it, those who seek truth will have reason to consider it, and those who reject it will have reason to regret it (and hopefully take time to reconsider).

Putting the Pieces Together
G. K. Chesterton became convinced that Christianity was true and reflective of the real world based on "an enormous accumulation of small but unanimous facts."[53] Certainly Chesterton's faith was built on more than his intellect, but this reasonable foundation gave him tremendous confidence in the truth of the gospel and enabled him to successfully share his faith with others. Chesterton effectively used a jigsaw guide to making sense of the world to anchor his belief and undercut popular arguments that life's big questions were too hard or too heavy. On the contrary, ultimate answers are available, and while people have different levels of access to the world there is sufficient evidence—within the world and within us—to point us in the right direction (see Rom 1:20). Identify things that stand out in the world, start putting the pieces together, and when you have enough pieces of the puzzle in place you can be confident that you see the big picture.

The jigsaw illustrates how every big-picture belief is the sum of many parts, and I was reminded of this when Sheryl and I had dinner with our good friends Brian and Shari McAlpine. As we sat together in their home I could not help commenting on an impressive painting on the wall, only for Brian to smile and point out, "It's a jigsaw." From a distance this painting appeared as one solid piece of art but moving closer revealed that it was made up of thousands of little pieces put together. Brian and his son Ian had demonstrated great patience and perseverance working on this puzzle, and the more they snapped things into place the more the image took shape and blended together. Similarly, every worldview is the sum of many parts, and when we understand how beliefs break down we will be better equipped to try and put them back together.

My wife, Sheryl, has a good friend Kate who was interested in talking about things that really matter. She had a lot of questions, and Sheryl encouraged her to use a jigsaw guide to making sense of the world. Kate began looking at life and putting the pieces together, and she clearly connected with the Christian worldview. It matched her expectations that life ought to have value, meaning and purpose. As her interest grew, Kate began reading the Bible, and she learned more about how questions of value, meaning and purpose are woven into the life, death and resurrection of Jesus Christ. The Christian worldview provides a context that makes sense of our experience, but it also challenges us to make a personal response to God, trusting in Jesus with our hearts, minds and souls. Kate was starting to see the big picture, and as God stirred her at a deeper level she made the decision to take a step of faith and trust in Jesus Christ.

A jigsaw guide to making sense of the world is a strategy that comes naturally, but we need to be prepared to overcome some of the common obstacles to putting it into practice. Every Christian can expect resistance to the Christian worldview, but when we prayerfully and practically do our best, we can trust God to draw people closer to the truth.

Summary

A jigsaw guide to making sense of the world will not answer every question, but it will help you start putting the pieces together so you can make sense of this broken world and see the big picture. Listen before you leap into a conversation that counts, learn to talk about things that really matter and be prepared to share the reason why the Christian worldview resonates with reality.

Discussion

What broken pieces of the world stand out and get your attention, and how could you use the Christian worldview to explain how these things fit together and paint the big picture?

A jigsaw strategy encourages you to think big by starting small. Where would you start when it comes to helping someone make sense of the world?

Recommended Reading

G. K. Chesterton. *Orthodoxy*. Colorado Springs: Shaw, 2001.

C. S. Lewis. *Mere Christianity*. New York: Scribner, 1952.

2

TRUTH

Be Prepared to Handle It

*"I can't share the truth about Christianity
because people get offended."*

"You mean you're a Christian?"

"Yes, and—"

"Well, I have a hard time with Christianity."

"Really, what's the problem?"

*"Don't you believe you're right and
everyone else is wrong?"*

If you identify yourself as a Christian, you may get stuck
with a label that describes you as harsh and offensive, and when
you try to stand up for your faith you will be told to sit down. It
can come as a shock that people find your belief so corrosive, but
the source of the problem is the cornerstone of Christian faith:
you claim to know the truth. To say your understanding of the
world is absolutely true means you believe you are right and everyone who disagrees with you is wrong. This is currently viewed as

the ultimate statement of arrogance. People are permitted to say they know what is true for them, but no one dare say they know what is true for everyone.

The culture rules that we each see the world from one (limited) perspective so we have no right to comment on what other people believe. Truth doesn't represent "what is" but only "what you think it is." Francis Schaeffer has said, "If there is no absolute beyond man's ideals, then there is no final appeal to judge between individuals and groups whose moral judgments conflict. We are merely left with conflicting opinions."[1] If no one has access to the truth, no one can speak with real authority, particularly on moral and metaphysical matters—e.g., right and wrong, God's existence and the meaning of life—and no one has a right to claim to know the truth because truth is out of reach.

Clearly Christians view the world very differently, and all believers need to be prepared to defend the reason they believe that truth is absolute, available and true—for everyone. This is the foundation for the Christian worldview and motivation for sharing the gospel. However, in the face of stinging criticism many Christians prefer to keep their head down and mouth closed, thinking, "I can't share my faith because people get offended." Certainly no one likes to get shot down and excluded from polite conversation, but there is no opt-out clause for Christians who would rather follow the path of least resistance. Instead God wants us to learn to handle the truth so we can stand up for our faith and offer a reasonable reply to those who bristle at our belief (1 Pet 3:15).[2]

A Brief Look at History
Truth has been under attack from the beginning of human history (see Gen 3 and following), so it's no surprise that people are still trying to resist, avoid and manipulate it. However, more recent cultural influences have even more severely contributed to the truth decay we see today. In the seventeenth century the phrase

Cogito ergo sum ("I think therefore I am") was coined by French philosopher René Descartes, and it is still used to promote the idea that you cannot be sure unless you are absolutely certain. Descartes was a brilliant philosopher who wanted to establish his beliefs on a firm foundation, so he started digging (and digging) and rejecting everything tainted with doubt. This process led Descartes to question everything until he was not certain of anything apart from his existence—he concluded he must exist in order to be able to ask the question "Do I exist?"[3]

The holy grail of Cartesian certainty suggests that one must dissolve all doubt before arriving at the truth. In practice this approach only encourages a steady slide into skepticism.[4] The problem is that we cannot be that sure about anything because we are fallible creatures, and Descartes set the bar too high, placing reasonable belief out of reach.

Scottish philosopher David Hume is widely recognized as one of the most significant influences in the history of Western thought. He wrote in the eighteenth century that reason will always fall short of producing belief so strong that it cannot be undermined, and as a result skepticism is inevitable.[5] If our beliefs are merely the result of how we see the world, then doubt squirts into everything and clouds our perception, so skepticism is preferable because it allows us to stop short of committing ourselves and making a big mistake. Hume was not the first to highlight the difficulty of grasping objective truth in a world where everything we know is subject to our experience, but his name remains popular among those who believe that the most reasonable option is to stand back and sit on the fence.

In the nineteenth and twentieth centuries modernity became the driving force in the search for concrete answers, and the scientific method was elevated and celebrated as the way to uncover truth about the world. There is no doubt that science helps us glean information about the natural world, but when it is trum-

peted as the tool to discover the truth about ultimate reality, it
turns into scientism and runs into problems, as Nicholas Rescher
has pointed out:

> The theorist who maintains that science is the be-all and
> end-all—that what is not in science textbooks is not worth
> knowing—is an ideologist with a peculiar and distorted
> doctrine of his own. For him, science is no longer a sector of
> the cognitive enterprise but an all-inclusive world-view. This
> is the doctrine not of science but of scientism. To take this
> stance is not to celebrate science but to distort it.[6]

Clearly this moves beyond investigating the natural world to
ruling out the existence of the supernatural world, and it does so
on the basis that there is no good evidence for it.[7] However, "good
evidence" is equated with direct physical evidence, and you cannot
find direct physical evidence for a nonphysical world by definition. So the supernatural is written off, which is like saying, "I
will believe in an invisible God only when I can see him."

If you do not directly apprehend something you still have good
reason to believe it exists when the indirect evidence points to it.
My young daughters grasp the simple illustration used by evangelist Billy Graham to defend reasonable belief in the existence of
God: you may not see the wind but you have good reason to believe it exists when you see its effect. Certainly there are ways to
empirically measure wind, something you cannot do in relation to
God's existence, but when you have an open mind simple observation is reason enough to sway you in the right direction. Good
science does not begin by ruling out the existence of the supernatural world, and many early heroes of the scientific method believed that a supernatural mechanic was necessary to explain the
complex mechanism of the universe.[8]

Another difficulty for those who claim that "science is the test
for everything" is that this statement is self-defeating; it cannot be

scientifically tested. You do not discover that "science is the test for everything" on the basis of examining the evidence. You assume it is true before you begin your investigation. Scientism is unscientific,[9] and its inability to make sense of the world means it is a worldview that is stumbling and crumbling.

The failure of modernity to make sense of reality bled into the twentieth and twenty-first centuries and encouraged the slide into postmodernity, in which truth is viewed as out of reach and everything is relative.[10] The focus is no longer on how the world is but on how we see the world—e.g., life is like being born with a set of uniquely tinted contact lenses glued to your eyeballs; you do not see the world as it is but only as it appears to be.

This belief has roots in philosophy, but its rapid cultural acceptance owes more to the fact that it proves wonderfully convenient. Instead of facing the pressure to conform to reality, you assume reality conforms to you. Do not work hard to establish what is true and the right thing to do; simply do what comes naturally and describe it as true and the right thing to do—for you. This sounds great in theory but it breaks down in practice: The New York Times gives a more grounded understanding of what this looks like in the real world when it reports cases of people who live side by side and struggle to get along. Countless articles and complaints about other people's noise remind us that lives overlap, worldviews collide and conflict is inevitable.[11]

The pages of history catalog society's leaning toward skepticism and disagreement, and many people suggest that Christians have lost the battle for truth. However, it's important to know that truth is shaken but not stirred. Descartes has not damaged it, Hume has not humbled it, modernity has not manipulated it, and postmodernity has not polluted it. Truth survives because truth can take care of itself. We do not really fight for truth but for an accurate understanding of truth, and we cannot allow it to be eroded from the popular culture. Truth is the cornerstone of belief, and

God wants Christians to stand up and defend its importance as the foundation for faith and the anchor for Christianity.

Establish the Meaning of the Word *Truth*

The word *truth* has been so abused that we need to reestablish what we mean by it, and I will use what could be called a traditional understanding from William Lane Craig: "A statement or proposition is (objectively) true if and only if it corresponds to reality."[12] Truth is what reflects the real world. If something is true it lines up with the way the world really is, and it is important to add that truth can be known. The experience of life is not like being born with uniquely tinted contact lenses glued to your eyeballs, but you could say we are born with different degrees of shortsightedness. Some things appear confusing because they are out of focus, but other things are clearly within reach.

Skeptics tend to focus on our limitations and put a question mark at the end of every sentence, as Joseph Natoli states: "The point is we cannot be absolute about the correspondence we make between our truth-claims and what might be true."[13] But even the most hardened skeptic will indirectly acknowledge that we can know that some things are true and reflect the real world. Consider a day in the life of a skeptic, from eating breakfast to crossing the road, and you realize that reality comes into focus at regular intervals. James Sire quotes theologian Robert Farrar Capon: "The skeptic is never for real. There he stands, cocktail in hand, left arm draped on the mantelpiece, telling you he can't be sure of anything, not even of his own existence. I'll give you my secret method of demolishing universal skepticism in four words. Whisper to him: 'Your fly is open.'"[14]

A generally accepted understanding of truth is under pressure, but we need to ask if public opinion carries enough weight to erase truth or redefine it. There is no doubt that popular culture has the power to morph the meaning of a word over time—for example, consider the statement "Our church minister lives a gay lifestyle." The prominent definition of the word *gay* may have changed, but this is simply semantics. The reality of its meaning "a cheery disposition" remains the same. You cannot erase what stands behind a word, even if you do not like it, because the essence of what a word stands for is out of reach. Letters that conjoin to form the word *truth* can be hijacked and reused to denote relativity, but there is no damage done to the traditional underlying meaning. We can still identify what truth stands for—for example, we could use the word *sploof* to represent the way things really are—and the meaning remains the same.

Regardless of the fact that truth corresponds to reality, people still try to ignore it and create their own version of the world they want to live in. However, what sounds ideal soon runs into trouble. There is no escaping the fact that many things in life are out of our control—the nature of the physical world, our health, the behavior of other people and so on. We do not have the power to create the world around us because it has already been created. Yet some people refuse to be put off. The idea of a DIY world is so attractive that they will defend it at all costs. Some return to the argument that we all see the world through different lenses, or perhaps they state that there are no lenses at all. The story of the blind men and the elephant suggests this latter approach, and it has been used to illustrate how human imperfection prevents us from seeing and knowing the whole truth.

Here is the story. A group of blind men who have never seen an elephant try to describe what the animal looks like after reaching out and touching it. One holds the tail and says an elephant is like a rope. Another feels the leg and argues it is like a tree. In each case no one seems capable of grasping the whole truth about the animal. The reason? Blind men have a limited grasp of reality. This story strikes a chord with us because we all have our "blind spots," but does this mean we cannot discover the truth about the world? Do our imperfections prevent us from seeing the big picture?

A closer examination of the story suggests otherwise, confirming the fact that truth exists independently of us. No matter what the blind men believe, it does not change the facts about the elephant. The story also reinforces the idea that we can know the truth. The blind men fall short, but the narrator (albeit more subtly) is able to put the pieces together. He can apparently see the big picture of the elephant, despite his limitations, and blind spots do not automatically prevent us from eventually grasping the true nature of reality.

Deal with Denial

The popular slogan "Denial is not a river in Egypt" can be aimed at those who seem determined to reject truth at all costs, even when it smacks them in the face. This gentle rebuke targets a kind of unblinking and unthinking denial of reality that makes us shake our heads in amazement, but the story of the emperor's new clothes reminds us that we can all resort to stubborn denial in the face of an uncomfortable truth: When two crooks pretended to make the emperor a special set of clothes that only the wisest people could see, of course there were no clothes, but no one was willing to admit this and be labeled a fool. In the end it took the courage of a young boy to break the dam of self-deception, and reality painfully poured in.

This story is known around the world because it resonates with something deep inside all of us. We recognize that there is truth; we want to know the truth; we feel pressure to believe the truth; but we can choose to deny the truth—for a variety of reasons. As Stephen T. Davis asserts, "We know what's right and wrong but wish we didn't, and we try to keep ourselves in ignorance so that we can do as we please."[15] The pressure to conform remains, but "few arguments possess irresistible force; few coerce people on pain of irrationality, so to speak, into accepting their conclusions. . . . It is always possible to find some reason to reject an argument whose conclusion one finds repugnant."[16]

George MacDonald was a nineteenth-century Christian minister and writer of fiction who went on to inspire many other authors of greater fame—W. H. Auden, C. S. Lewis and J. R. R. Tolkien among them. MacDonald creatively communicated the benefit of a Christian perspective, and he has been described as a man who "had an intensive desire to know the truth . . . [and] once found, his consuming passion was to order his daily life according to that truth." Certainly this is the way we ought to be, but Frederick Suppe, another Christian philosopher, reminds us of a more base inclination. In practice "one stakes out one's philosophical position and *then* seeks arguments in its defense—to rationalize the previously determined conviction."[17]

The BBC television program *Can't Take It with You* featured a Muslim couple who struggled to come to terms with the Qur'an's teaching on inheritance. After speaking to a series of scholars they managed to find one who gave them enough wiggle room to do what they wanted. I do not mean to sound cruel, since the conversations were clearly heartfelt and the couple seemed eager to do the right thing—and to be seen to do the right thing. However, the driving force was not to fall into line with the Qur'an but to find someone who would make the Qur'an fall into line with them. Eventually they found a friendly face—and a flexible scholar— willing to interpret the text in a more comfortable way, and the program's happy ending was a couple able to do what they wanted and believe it was the right thing.

Living in denial of the truth sounds attractive if it means you get to do what you want, but it comes at a cost. No one will respect you if you are seen to deliberately deceive yourself, and to appear to deceive others is a serious stain on your character. In fact, public sentiment is so strong that you dare not call someone a liar, even if it is widely acknowledged that the person habitually does not tell the truth. It is almost comical to hear the popular euphemisms "He's economical with the truth," or "She isn't entirely honest," and these catch phrases are used to soften the blow. Obviously there are pragmatic reasons to discourage lying, and society could not function if we could not generally believe anything people told us. You could not purchase goods with confidence, rely on others to respect your property or perform the most basic tasks such as getting on a bus without wondering, "Where is the driver *really* taking me?" Lying causes a breakdown in the structure of our society, and on a more personal level it sends us on a downward spiral. One lie needs another to cover it up, and as Abraham Lincoln reportedly said, "No man has a good enough memory to be a successful liar." Keeping up with the consequences of telling a lie brings anxiety and discomfort, and even if we get away with it we feel something burning inside. We seem to be wired to tell the truth—even if this wiring is often faulty—and when someone argues that they know a person who is entirely unruffled about lying, tell them to ask this person, "Are you a liar?" to discover the truth.

Living a lie is complicated and confusing, but clearly there are times it seems be to our advantage. Many people are even encouraged to live a lie when it allows them to do what they want. However, people are not satisfied with doing what they want; they need to feel they are doing what is right. So it falls on the rest of us to make them feel like their belief is true and the right thing to do. We are told to affirm everyone. Instead of disagreeing, we must applaud them to make them feel better about themselves.

The story of the emperor's new clothes, however, reminds us that you cannot make something true simply by affirming it, no matter how hard you try. When this becomes obvious, many people try to go in the opposite direction. If we cannot elevate all beliefs to the level where everything is true, the alternative is to relegate all beliefs to the level where nothing is true. This tackles the problem a different way with the same result: we can do what we want and feel good about it because there is no higher truth to challenge us. However, those who choose to deny that anything is true end up contradicting themselves and proving there is truth after all.

Consider the proposition "there is no truth." If this is true—that there is no truth—obviously something is true, and the claim defeats itself because "there is no truth" is true—and truth exists. Alternately, if "there is no truth" is false, then "there is truth" must be true—and truth still exists. Either way, claiming "there is no truth" simply ends up proving that there is truth after all. The next time you hear someone claim there is no truth just ask, "Is that true, that there is no truth?" Hopefully they will get the point that it takes the truth to deny the truth, and those who persist merely undermine their own position and end up sawing off the branch they are sitting on.[18]

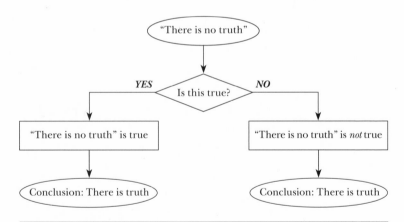

Figure 2.1. Truth is undeniable

Deal with Disagreement

Truth is often avoided whenever it is awkward or uncomfortable, but another reason truth claims are unpopular relates to the fact that they are exclusive and provoke disagreement. Exclusivity and disagreement are viewed very negatively in our society, and the culture tries to promote a more inclusive approach to everything. We are encouraged to agree with other people, even those we disagree with. We may believe others are not right but we must not say we believe they are wrong, since who are we to make this kind of judgment? Apart from being naive, this suggestion is nonsense. Truth is exclusive by definition, and you cannot agree with those you disagree with since you disagree with them.

In fact, we could not function on an everyday level without embracing the exclusive nature of truth. Imagine a politician who refused to exclusively present himself as the best candidate. Consider a salesman who denied the exclusive appeal of his product. What about a doctor who made her diagnosis and then put it on a par with everyone who disagreed with her? People make exclusive claims all the time, and every time you claim to know the truth you automatically exclude every belief that contradicts your belief (note: you don't exclude the person). To say you believe that something is true means you believe that it corresponds to reality, and anything that contradicts this claim is deemed false because it does not correspond to reality. When it comes to truth and falsehood, it is either one or the other. There is no middle ground.

The law of noncontradiction. The first lesson of classical logic is "A is A, and A is not non-A."[19] This is the law of noncontradiction: nothing can be both A and non-A at the same time. For example, either my wife, Sheryl, is pregnant or my wife,

$$A \neq \text{Non-A}$$

Figure 2.2. The law of noncontradiction

Sheryl, is not pregnant; there is no middle ground. The belief that she is pregnant is either true or false, and she cannot be both pregnant and not pregnant at the same time.

We readily embrace this law without thinking about it, and we could not function without it, but some people argue that it is wrong. Yet the argument against the law of noncontradiction ends up using the law of noncontradiction. R. C. Sproul states, "Augustine also argued that the law of noncontradiction cannot be disputed, for it must be assumed and employed in every effort to deny it."[20] In seeking to deny this law we are presented with a choice: either we should use the law or we should reject the law (it is not a case of both using the law and rejecting the law), and in case you missed it, the exclusive law has been smuggled back into the equation.

When things don't make sense. There are situations where our feelings pull us in different directions—for example, a prospective father may describe himself as happy and unhappy at the same time. There are also supernatural claims that appear to be mutually exclusive. This is certainly true about some important aspects of biblical Christianity, and it is one reason people often point the finger and say it does not make sense. Scottish comedian Billy Connolly, who is able to put a smile on the face of most people, got my serious attention when he referred to one of the difficult things Jesus said while being interviewed by British television host Michael Parkinson: "You know when they say those things, that Christians say all the time? 'I am one in him, and he is one in me.' Explain! I don't get it! . . . What? He's his own father? What's happening here?" I admit that I was delighted to hear him express this question, and I regret that he grew up in a Christian context where he was not encouraged to raise his hand when he scratched his head. If only we could turn back the clock and turn to the verse that communicates this truth (Jn 10:38), we could encourage him to see that the context sheds light on the situation.

One myth about the Bible is that it's full of people who were prepared to believe anything since they were a little backward back then. Because they lacked the scientific progress of a more enlightened society like ours, we have to assume that the ancients were simply gullible. C. S. Lewis called this chronological snobbery,[21] and if you read the Bible (or history), you discover that this is not the case. Jesus was not buoyed by easy belief; he was cut to the heart by constant criticism. Even those closest to him, such as the apostle Thomas, struggled to believe in him (Jn 20:25).

Consider the verse Connolly was referring to. Jesus was speaking directly to those who didn't get it. He was claiming to be God, but note what he said to back this up: "Even though you do not believe me, believe the miracles, that you may know and understand that the Father is in me, and I in the Father" (Jn 10:38). What was Jesus doing? He was using a jigsaw strategy to help people make sense of a difficult situation. When we are confronted by pieces of a puzzle that do not seem to fit or make sense, we can stand back and see what else is snapping into place. Jesus was performing miracles on a scale never seen before, and even his fiercest critics could not dispute this. They could only argue that he was working in the power of the devil (Mt 9:34). The miracles established his credibility (Lk 3:14-21) and pushed the boundaries of credulity, helping people believe this man was no ordinary man because he was the God-man. People then as now had no category for this, so they were encouraged to lean on the things they did know in order to see more of the big picture.

Billy Connolly, or anyone who is asking these questions, could think of examples a little closer to home. Maybe there was a time Connolly's wife told him something she was terribly serious about, but it seemed outrageous to him. Yet he was willing to believe her—even when it did not make sense. Why? Because his confusion was outweighed by the fact that his wife had enough credibility in his eyes he was sometimes willing to believe the unbelievable. When it comes to believing anything, the power of testimony cannot be overstated. Think about many of the important things you believe. You know them on the basis that someone else told you about them. The decision to accept a person's testimony comes down to credibility. Is the source trustworthy? There are many times in life when we will be confronted by things that don't seem to make sense, and a jigsaw guide to making sense of the world helps us overcome them by allowing us to stand back and think about what else snaps into place.

When I hear people like Billy Connolly say they know what Jesus said and shake their head in amazement because it seems like madness, I start to get excited about the conversation. Peter Kreeft, a professor of philosophy at Boston College, explains, "The non-Christian who thinks Christians are insane is far closer to Christian faith than the non-Christian who thinks Christians are just nice people."[22] When the Bible or Jesus makes claims that I do not understand it does not instantly trouble me. It would worry me more if the infinite wonder of God could comfortably fit inside a finite human head. But I do not use this as an excuse. These same sources claim there are still good reasons to believe, so when we come across something that seems like a logical contradiction, we don't have to immediately throw in the towel. We can deal with the difficulty, just as we would in any area of life, by thinking about what else snaps into place.

Jesus certainly claimed to be God, which is outrageous if it is not true, and that is why the Jewish leaders were prepared to stone him for blasphemy (Jn 8:58-59). However, other aspects of Jesus' life reinforce this claim and offer reasons to believe it. Consider the life he lived, the death he died, his resurrection from the dead. Take notice of the impact of his life on people for two thousand years in every culture and every continent. These are areas people can investigate to see if things add up, and we ought to give Jesus a reasonable opportunity to establish himself as a credible authority. This is more than a research project. If the Bible is true, there will be supernatural forces at work in the life of anyone who is genuinely looking for answers. A stirring in the heart, mind and soul as they start to see the big picture, and when they have enough pieces in place they can look an apparent logical contradiction in the eye and still know they have good reason to believe Christianity is true.

Using the law of noncontradiction against Christian belief is effective only if it turns everything upside-down, but the more you examine the evidence the more you discover that Jesus turns the world the right-way-up. There are many philosophical, historical, archaeological, intellectual, relational and personal reasons to believe in it—and to believe in him.

The Truth About Tolerance

Another attempt to override truth is to demand that people agree with you—and to define this as tolerance. We see this in the popular culture when we dare to suggest that someone holds a belief that is wrong, particularly on a sensitive moral issue. We are likely to be shouted down and labeled intolerant. This is bizarre since we do not need to tolerate those we agree with—after all, we agree with them. Tolerance is meant for those we disagree with— we agree to disagree while remaining agreeable. Tolerance means respecting others and allowing them the right to hold and express their views. The true spirit of tolerance does not close mouths; it opens them. As Phillip E. Johnson has said, "Relativism about truth does not lead to tolerance. Rather, it leads to the conclusion that social conflicts cannot be resolved by reason or even compromise, because there is no common reason that can unite groups that differ on fundamental questions."[23] The new "tolerance" demands that if you have nothing supportive to say it is best to say nothing at all—in other words, you will not be tolerated.

When popular radio host Laura Schlessinger was outspoken in her views against homosexuality, claiming she believed it to be morally wrong, there was a storm of public protest.[24] A television news report showed people demonstrating, trying to make the case that Schlessinger had no right to hold and express these views. Curiously, it was presented as a fight for tolerance by the protestors who were standing against the intolerance of Schlessinger. In reality, the protestors were the ones being intolerant of her by not allowing her to hold and express her views, and she was actually demonstrating tolerance toward them. Schlessinger disagreed with them but respected their right to hold and express their views. Our topsy-turvy society is confused on this issue, and many are trying to promote tolerance by demonstrating intolerance toward anyone who disagrees with them. This is a dangerous trend because it threatens our right to stand up for what we believe and speak out about the truth.

Before we move on it's worth noting that Christianity is regularly singled out as "exclusive," but the fact is that every religion, philosophy and worldview is exclusive. Every big picture claims to represent the truth. Islam is based on the belief the Qur'an is God's word, and if you contradict its teaching your belief is excluded from the truth. Hinduism may appear to be more inclusive, but if you argue that there is only one God your position is excluded (for being too exclusive). Buddhism makes a number of claims about reality, but if you claim that following Jesus is the only way to discover the truth your belief will be excluded. Truth is at the core of every belief system, and when you claim to know the truth, those who disagree must by default believe what is false. There is no shame in this. Every truth claim is exclusive and results in disagreement, and our goal should be to demonstrate true tolerance by agreeing to disagree—with love, gentleness and respect.

I was challenged to put this into practice when asked to participate in a student conference on Islam. A Muslim and Hindu had already agreed to take part, and I was invited to provide a Christian perspective. I remembered some wise words from Ravi Zacharias who was invited into a classroom setting to directly criticize another religion: when you throw mud you only get your hands dirty and give up a lot of ground. So I tried to follow his lead and take a more constructive approach. I taught a couple of sessions in the morning and then everyone came together in the afternoon. At the end of the day there was a special presentation on Islam, followed by a panel discussion. The imam who spoke used a narrative style that was very engaging, but I was surprised to hear him describe Islam in broad, inclusive terms—for example, Muslims believe in the God of the Bible; Islam recognizes all the biblical prophets; Muslims have a deep respect for Jesus. What was meant to bring things to a satisfactory conclusion caused some confusion, so I was not surprised when the first question during the panel discussion was directed to me: "Why are you a Christian?" Why indeed? If we all believe the same thing, why do I choose to align myself with Christianity? I began by affirming my respect for each person on the panel, and then I briefly outlined some of the major differences between Islam and Christianity. Christians and Muslims ought to respect one another, but there is no doubt that these belief systems are mutually exclusive with radically different views on the nature of God, Scripture, Jesus Christ, salvation, sanctification, heaven and hell. The students listened—and learned—that interfaith dialogue tends to be built around reducing our beliefs to the lowest common denominator. It is driven by the desire to see everyone get along, but it merely sweeps the real differences under the carpet. The key to promoting meaningful discussion and demonstrating true tolerance is learning to appreciate our differences, respect other people's beliefs and warmly engage those who disagree with us.

Expose the Cultural Mechanism
Truth is unavoidable, undeniable and within reach, but we need to return to the question of how to grasp it. In chapter one the jigsaw was presented as a guide to knowing the truth and making sense of the world, but we need to expose a cultural myth that is the source of much confusion. If you turn on the TV or listen to the radio you will be encouraged to believe that you discover the truth by disengaging your mind and listening to your heart. Human reason is flawed, obviously, but somehow our feelings survive our imperfection and hold the key.

The popular *Lord of the Rings* film series includes a scene that carries this message (which no doubt has Tolkien turning in his grave). It happens during a hushed conversation between two main characters, Gandalf and Aragorn, who are discussing the well-being of Frodo, the hero of the story. Frodo is out of reach on a dangerous quest, and they wonder aloud whether he is dead or alive. Aragorn turns to Gandalf and poses the ultimate question: "What does your heart tell you?" Cue movie close-up, pregnant pause and dramatic climax with Gandalf's answer: "Frodo is alive!" The scene does not suggest that Gandalf is guided by supernatural insight (which he allegedly had access to), and instead we are left with the impression that the human heart holds the key.

Movies subtly reinforce a message by making us feel warm and fuzzy, but it is important to sober people with a bucket of cold reality. Consider another time, another place. Imagine my wife, Sheryl, asks me to run an errand, so I leave the house and notice our young son Asher playing in the garden. Sheryl is busy so I tell him to stay there until I get back. Fifteen minutes later I return and find his toys strangely abandoned. I walk inside and Sheryl tells me she has not seen him, so I continue to check around the house. I still cannot find Asher, and my heart is beating a little faster as I expand my search. I begin shouting his name and talking to our neighbors but no one can help. Eventually I run back to the house but Sheryl still has no idea where he could be, so I prepare to move into overdrive—until Sheryl holds out her hand and stops me in my tracks. She closes her eyes and after a moment's silence starts to smile, whispering, "Asher is fine, Asher is fine. . . . I just listened to my heart." What kind of father would I be if I breathed a sigh of relief, sat down and poured a cup of coffee? It will come as no surprise to find out I am not interested in what Sheryl's heart has to say about the matter. I want to know the truth about the safety of our son, and I will not rest until there is good reason to believe he is safe and sound.

You do not have to be a paranoid parent to realize Sheryl's imaginary reaction does not make sense—it is nonsense! Movie sentimentality sells a lot of popcorn but fails to satisfy us in the real world. When you are potentially facing a life-and-death situation, you do not want to listen to your heart; you want to know the truth. If a loved one is lost you want to know he is safe, and you will keep searching until you have good reason to believe it. If a child or parent develops troubling physical symptoms, you do not ignore them because a friend has a feeling that everything will be all right. You want the advice of a reliable doctor who can correctly diagnose the problem and help you find a solution. We do not disengage our minds and listen to our feelings when we want to know the truth about the world, but we are tempted to do so when we want to ignore it.

Establishing truth based on feelings alone is unreliable, but it's attractive because it allows us to believe what we feel and do what we want. We cannot really be criticized for our feelings because we do not choose them; they choose us—they are what they are. As one musician in a rock band said, "If it feels good then you should go for it. I want to be remembered for being honest."[25] To preface a belief with "I feel . . ." makes a subtle appeal to critical immunity, and like producing a "get out of jail free" card you can sidestep those prepared to challenge you. "Hey, I never said it *is*. I just said I *feel* like it is." When truth grows out of our feelings, truth becomes comfortable, convenient, immune from criticism and, most importantly, ours!

However, a "truth is in the eye of the beholder" philosophy is less attractive when a friend tells you he believes something because he feels it's right and you have serious reservations. You don't want to pat him on the back; you want to steer him in the right direction. But when feelings are the sole currency for making a decision, there is nothing reasonable you can say that has the power to penetrate. What's worse, any decision to question your friend's feelings may be interpreted not as a sign of concern but as a lack of support.

There is a good illustration in the popular American television show *Friends* when Phoebe is convinced that a cat is carrying the spirit of her dead mother. The rest of the group quickly gather around her and affirm her, suggesting that's what friends are for. Ross is the only one who dares question Phoebe. He reasons that the cat is a cat (one that belongs to a little girl in the neighborhood), so he tries to stand up for the truth but is instantly shot down and alienated by the others. The message is clear and comes straight from the mouth of Phoebe: you are not a real friend unless you're willing to offer unquestioning support for another's beliefs, no matter what those beliefs are. In the end the cat is returned to avoid upsetting the little girl, but the tragedy is that Ross concedes defeat and lines up with the others—even apologizing to the cat.

It sounds wonderful to have friends who are so supportive, putting your feelings before everything else. However, before we draw any hasty conclusions, we should contrast this with an imaginary episode. Phoebe finds a black cat and believes this is such bad luck that she needs to end her life by jumping off the roof of the apartment building. Would the viewers be laughing as everyone gathered around her and supported her, offering to hold her coat (and the cat) as she jumped? Would they turn on Ross if he questioned her decision and failed to support her by daring to offer reasons she should choose to live? If this episode aired you can be sure her friends would immediately question the legitimacy of Phoebe's feelings and try to get her to grasp the true picture of reality. They would argue that her life was valuable and continue to support her until her feelings changed to reflect the truth. The relative realm of feelings does not consistently reflect the real world, and we should never manipulate truth to be in line with our feelings. Often we need to bring our feelings back into line with what is true.

Feelings are wonderful and God-given—a primary source of joy, inspiration and information in our lives. God directs us and affects us with his love, joy and peace, but feelings are not designed to be isolated and used as our primary truth-telling mechanism.

Os Guinness is a popular author and sought-after social critic who has remarked, "In the Bible, *heart* can be translated as emotions in only a fraction of its many hundreds of uses. In the overwhelming majority of cases, it makes nonsense of the passage to translate it this way. Understood biblically, heart refers to the seat of the whole human person, the true self. In most cases, it refers to our understanding and not our emotions."[26] Please understand that I am not criticizing feelings, but I am warning against the popular culture mindset that uses them alone to determine the truth. We cannot afford to default to feelings or unquestioningly support someone who claims to be guided by them. Sometimes feelings need to stand corrected and be brought back into line with reality, and sometimes it's a real friend who is willing to come alongside you—and hurt your feelings—by speaking the truth.

Counter the Contradictions
Before we bring this chapter on truth to a close I want to briefly return to the importance of responding to popular contradictions. When people claim that truth does not exist (or that we cannot grasp it), gently point out that this is a self-contradiction but also underline the fact that no one lives like they believe this. To open your mouth and speak with any sense or authority suggests that you believe that what you say is true—for other people, too; otherwise why say it? Can you imagine someone disputing everything she said? It would make no sense. We assume that most of the things we say correspond to reality. For example, when you ask someone what he had for breakfast you tend to believe the answer is true and that the person believes it to be true. However, self-contradictions continue to arise and need to be pointed out, sensitively, particularly when they are used to stop Christians from sharing their faith.

"You can't talk about religion!" is a classic example that needs to be exposed because it presents a double-whammy. The person who makes this statement clearly is allowed to talk about religion (note that religion is the subject of the sentence), but he denies others the right to do the same. So instead of taking this on the chin and taking your seat, thank the person for indirectly agreeing with you—that you can talk about religion since he just did. Then feel free to present your own, more tolerant view on the subject and defend the right of others to talk about religion and have their say. Thomas Morris recounts, "A man once said to me that he had been told all his life there were three topics that should not be talked about in polite company: religion, sex and politics. He then went on to add that the older he got, the more he came to realize that these were the only things worth talking about."[27]

"You can't tell people what to believe!" is another protest to watch out for. Sometimes blurted out as a conversation stopper, this remark can be used as a direct attack on evangelism. At first it seems like an innocent attempt to stand against pushy religious types, but whoever says this is telling others (you) what to believe, something she just said should not be done. She is being a pushy nonreligious type. We do not want to encourage people to be pushy, whether religious or nonreligious, but there is nothing wrong with telling other people what to believe. We do it nearly every time we open our mouth and speak intelligibly: I prefer coffee over tea; it's raining outside; world hunger is a problem and we should do something about it; you should look both ways before crossing the road. In each case I am telling you what to believe, but this is not the same as making you believe it. You have to decide whether or not you believe it to be true. The issue is not telling other people what to believe but making sure we do so with the right attitude.

Sharing the Christian faith depends on the freedom to speak, so the most direct way to blunt it and stunt it is to tell Christians to keep quiet. However, the person who says everyone should close his or her mouth will always open his own, so if all things are equal (which is the crux of the matter—usually they are not), you should have the right to do the same. Learning to respond to popular examples of self-refutation will help you overcome common criticisms of Christianity, and you will be better equipped to defend your right to share your faith and tell other people what to believe. Our attitude is key, since we want to build others up, not knock them down, and while some will reject what you say, at least you will get the conversation back on track and put truth back on the table.

Standing on a Firm Foundation
I have posed this question to many Christian groups I've worked with: "What is the most important thing about Christianity?" The responses are what you would expect: the love of God, the cross of Christ, the resurrection of Jesus and so on. In each case I deliberately keep the conversation going to prove an important point: "Yes, that is very important, but it is not the *most* important." Soon the atmosphere begins to change. I hear rumblings of discontent because this is not what people expected. I normally have to step in to break the tension, and I can win a rare moment of silence when I whisper one word that provides the answer: "Truth!"

Christianity stands or falls on whether or not it is true; every powerful claim about Christianity crumbles if it is false. Yet to say that truth is the most important thing about Christianity surprises people. In fact, it makes many Christians uncomfortable. It seems to relegate the position and authority of Jesus Christ, and I appreciate this concern, but we need to understand that Jesus himself understood the importance of truth. We are not placing truth over and above Jesus Christ, we are grounding truth in him. Two thousand years ago Pilate questioned Jesus of Nazareth and asked, "What is truth?" Jesus said, "I am the way and the truth and the life" (Jn 14:6). He is the cornerstone of Christianity because he is the very essence of truth. His life, death, resurrection and ascension correspond to reality and help us make sense of the world. Os Guinness puts it like this: "The Christian faith is not true because it works. It works because it is true."[28] There are many wonderful things to treasure about Christianity but each loses its luster if it is not true. That is why the movement to undermine truth is perhaps the greatest threat to the proclamation and defense of the Christian faith.

Some people are unmoved by this kind of discussion because they believe the intellectual defense of Christianity is unnecessary and Christian apologetics is unwanted (if not unwarranted). I once contacted a respected Christian leader to share about the ministry of Reason Why, offering to meet and see if there was a way we could work together. His reply made it clear that the door was closed and the conversation was over: "I am sorry to be so blunt, but I can't see us utilizing your resources, and therefore don't want to waste your time beating around the bush. I am sure they are excellent, and other churches and groups will hugely benefit from them, but they are not for us at this time." Many Christians fail to appreciate that truth is pivotal when it comes to developing a confident belief and sharing it with others.

Truth is also important during times of testing and trial. Christian living often seems to lack the fringe benefits we would expect. When difficult circumstances threaten to drag us down, our confidence in the truth can pull us through. Christian faith is not secured in our experience or tied to our circumstances; it is anchored in the truth. Christ's claim to be the truth means his message is for all people at all times, and that is why it should concern us to see truth diminished in our culture. It should be of even greater concern to see truth diminished in our churches, because when you erode the pillar of truth you shake the very foundation of Christianity.

Christianity stands or falls on the answer to the question "Is it true?" and the apostle Paul—whose life was transformed when he encountered the risen Jesus Christ—said if the resurrection of

Christ is not true, if it did not really happen, then the Christian faith has no value. We are simply deluding ourselves and "to be pitied more than all men" (1 Cor 15:12-19). Truth is essential to Christian belief, and that means it is worth fighting for. Do not apologize for it, deny it or try to disguise it, but remember to speak the truth in love when the time comes to defend it. What you say can be overshadowed by the way you say it, and the apostle Peter reminds us to share the reason for the hope that we have with gentleness and respect (1 Pet 3:15). Action is important but attitude is key, and when you understand this principle and can put it into practice, you are ready to handle the truth.

Summary

The Christian worldview is built on the foundation of truth, God wants us to know the truth, and we need to be prepared to handle the truth so we can offer a reasonable reply to those who bristle at our belief. Jesus Christ claimed to be the truth, and when we understand the reason why, we will know why this message is for all people at all times and in all places.

Discussion

Have you encountered people who are uncomfortable with anyone claiming to know the truth? If so, how could you help steer them in the right direction?

What do people generally think about truth and tolerance, and what could you say to clear up some of the confusion?

Recommended Reading

Nancy Pearcey. *Total Truth*. Wheaton, Ill.: Crossway, 2004.

Douglas Groothuis. *Truth Decay: Defending Christianity Against the Challenges of Postmodernism*. Downers Grove, Ill.: InterVarsity Press, 2000.

3

BELIEF

Be Prepared to Share It

"I don't like Christians—they're too pushy!"

"What do you mean?"

"They're always telling other people what to believe."

*"But don't they have the right to share their
beliefs with other people?"*

*"No! Everyone should be left alone
to believe what they want."*

I sensed the tension and uncertainty in the room as I stood before a group of students. My host had not done me any favors, introducing me as "the Christian speaker," and I could almost see the invisible barriers rising before I had a chance to open my mouth. Christians have a reputation for ruffling feathers. They are assumed to be pushy and pretentious, and the students had their mental and emotional shields in place, ready to deflect whatever I said. However, instead of launching into a Christian monologue, telling them what they should believe, I started asking questions.

People naturally demonstrate resistance to anyone who challenges the way they look at the world because they understand that it will impact the way they live. So when you prepare to discuss the Christian worldview in an environment where people are guarded, it's a good idea to begin by asking questions. The Socratic method also allows us to dig deeper and discover what others believe and the reasons they believe it, and when you listen before you leap into a conversation, you can prepare to show sensitivity toward those who disagree with you. This is the basis for meaningful dialogue—although when you stand up for a Christian perspective, no matter how hard you try to avoid it you will tread on people's toes sooner or later.

As I worked with this group one student told me it's better not saying anything about what other people believe, using the contemporary language that "everyone should be left alone to believe what they want." I was not surprised to hear this, since it represents a popular outlook on life. The idea is that we ought to draw our own boundaries, each of us retreating into a bubble that protects our beliefs and prevents them from coming into conflict with anyone else. This kind of bubble theory sounds wonderful, and who would not want to live the dream of the fast-food hamburger—where you can have it your way? Unfortunately, like most bubbles, it bursts as soon as you try to take hold of it.

Bursting the Bubble

The bubble theory bursts for two main reasons. First, it's self-defeating. The person who says, "Everyone should be left alone to believe what they want" is not leaving other people alone to believe what they want. This individual has stepped outside his bubble of belief and walked directly into your bubble to tell you what to believe. He is calling for you to adjust your belief so it falls into line with his, all under the subtle guise of letting everyone believe what they want. Many people are quick to fall for this line—and fall into line—and as a result they are no longer prepared to stand up and stand out for what they believe. However, the next time someone says, "People should be left alone to believe what they want," you need to point out, "But you're not leaving me alone to believe what I want." Help others see that theirs is a self-defeating statement, the kind we considered in chapter two, and be ready to respond when people try to use it to get you to step back and not say anything.

The idea that we should be left alone to believe what we want is often described as making our own lifestyle choice, which has become something of a cultural cliché. Sheryl and I watched a television program that featured young people who embraced outlandish behavior, and the hosts were careful to preface their veiled critique with, "I respect your lifestyle choice, but . . ." It was bizarre to hear people say something about life outside their bubble while pretending to say nothing and remain inside their bubble. If you truly believe you have nothing to say about other people's beliefs you will keep your mouth closed. Unclench teeth at your peril, because speaking the words "We should stop trying to influence others" makes you immediately guilty of a contradiction: you are trying to influence others. People make such contradictory statements because they appreciate the benefits of an open mouth—and an open mind—and we ought to remind them of the advantages of another perspective.

The second reason the bubble theory bursts is that it is soul-destroying. The myth of Sisyphus tells of a man eternally condemned by the gods to roll a boulder up a hill only to see it roll back down again. Sisyphus faces a life of endless frustration. He is constantly reaching for a goal that cannot be realized. In a similar way the bubble theory suggests that we can pursue a life where we get to do what we want, but the reality is that we cannot because other people get in the way. Ravi Zacharias is one of the most powerful and gifted speakers on this subject, and he offers a vivid example in which this theory breaks down: "In some cultures people love their neighbors, in others they eat them."[1] Zacharias shatters the myth that left to our own devices we will all just get along. Reality bites (pardon the pun) when a family of hungry cannibals moves in next door.

Despite the difficulty of grounding morality in ourselves, the powerful attraction of a do-it-yourself life persists. The next move of the bubble theorist is to introduce the caveat "as long as you don't hurt anyone else." This is an admirable stance, but before we consider whether it's even practical, it's worth asking where this "rule" suddenly comes from and why we should believe or obey it. One minute it's up to us to decide our dos and don'ts, and then a universal law suddenly appears that we're supposed to obey. Clearly this is an attempt to smuggle in something authoritative, something above us and beyond us that provides a standard for what we ought to do, but there is no basis for it, at least not on this worldview.

The suggestion that we are not allowed to hurt anyone else directly contradicts the claim that we should not interfere with other people's beliefs. You may believe we should not hurt other people, but what if others believe differently? If we are consistent, we can support the "hurt clause" only for those who support the hurt clause; we must also support those who reject it on the basis that it is not right for them. The happy-go-lucky cannibal may smirk at the rule as she munches on her next-door neighbor, deciding that her lifestyle choice encourages her to reject it.

We cannot claim that we have the right to choose our own lifestyle and then introduce the clause "as long as we don't hurt anyone else." Either we have the right to choose or we don't. If we do, we are free to reject all clauses, including the "don't hurt anyone else" clause. However, let us ignore the implosion of this statement long enough to consider if we could live like this. Hurting someone means inflicting a degree of injury on another person, but why should it be restricted to physical hurt? What about emotional or psychological damage, which may have even deeper and longer-lasting effects? If we truly want to avoid hurting, we must stretch the definition far enough to include whatever seems to trouble others. If you introduce the hurt clause, your hope of living the good life is over. Your actions will be stymied every time someone says, "But you can't because that would hurt me!"

Building Belief

It is necessary to burst the bubble theory by popping the colorful idea that the world would be a better place if we just left people alone to believe what they want. Point out that those who say this are guilty of making a logical contradiction as well as advocating a practical impossibility. Be respectful when people say, "Everyone should keep their beliefs to themselves," but recognize that these people are not keeping their beliefs to themselves. Clear up the confusion and establish a platform that gives you the right to share your beliefs in the same way. Every belief offers insight into the way people engage the world, and if you want to be sure you are living in the real world you need to be able to secure your beliefs on a reasonable foundation.

Contrary to popular opinion, all beliefs are not created equal, and the best beliefs are those we have good reason to believe are true and correspond to reality. This is what it means to build your beliefs on a reasonable foundation. When it comes to life and the big picture, the general desire should be to know what is real (and really true), but this approach is often overruled by the attraction of whatever looks good, feels good, makes us comfortable, seems convenient or falls into line with other people. This is a dangerous way to live because it lacks real security, genuine stability and continuity, and we get a vivid picture of this when we turn to a memorable story told by a remarkable man.

Jesus is widely recognized, even among other religions, as one of the wisest individuals who ever lived. This comes as no surprise to Christians who believe what the Bible says: he is the God-man. So when Jesus speaks it is worth listening. Two thousand years ago he spoke on the importance of building your life on a strong foundation, using a parable to prove the point (Mt 7:24-27): There was a wise man and a foolish man. One man decided to build his house on rock, and the other chose to build his house on sand. When I teach on this passage I like to point out that a house on the beach sounds more appealing. Just think of the attraction of living on the water's edge: direct access to the waves and unrestricted views of the open water. However, a serious storm comes along and we start to see the significance of this parable. A popular television program called *Location, Location, Location* has claimed to know what's most important when buying a property, but Jesus counters this with foundation, foundation, foundation. A location looks good on a sunny day, but it's the foundation that decides whether you survive the storm. In the parable, the biblical text is clear that this is a savage storm, the kind likely to leave its mark, but the crucial point is the outcome. Both men experience the storm but only one has what it takes to survive. The house on the sand collapses; the house on the rock stands strong.

Translate this parable back into the real world and we can ask the question, are you building your life on a firm foundation? When it comes to building a worldview there is a great temptation to stand on whatever seems most attractive. Do this, Jesus said, and difficult times will bring you crashing down. Build your life on the truth of Jesus Christ and you will stand strong. The parable has double application, referring to this life and the life to come, which only makes it more significant. We need to make sure we are committed to him for today, tomorrow and for eternity.

Reason Why was launched as a ministry in Scotland, and as Sheryl and I began sharing in the early days, one family was quick to come alongside us. Andy and Eleanor were passionate about missions and actively supported God's work around the world, so when I learned that Andy was an accountant, I asked if he would be willing to serve on the board as treasurer. He agreed and we started meeting together, planning and discussing with the other board members how to put the financial structure in place. It was an exciting time. Sheryl and I were enjoying getting to know this couple and their family, and when Eleanor called one day just hearing her voice made me smile, until I realized her serious tone. Andy was very ill and was being admitted to the hospital.

We jumped into action and made arrangements to look after their two young children. Eleanor went to the hospital to be with her husband, and while we knew his condition was serious, we were cautiously optimistic that this fit and faithful young man would pull through. This only heightened our shock when he died two days later. Our thoughts immediately turned to Eleanor and the children, a godly young family hit by one of the most severe storms life can throw at you. In these circumstances many people crumble, yet the ongoing testimony of Eleanor's life is that of a beautiful woman standing strong. What is her remarkable secret? It is no secret. Eleanor has told many people and she would tell you: she stands only because she has built her life on the rock of Jesus Christ. Life is not easy, but she draws supernatural strength every day, and she experiences a deep sense of peace that the world does not understand.

Jesus told the story of the wise man and the foolish man to deal with a serious subject that demands our attention: when the storms of life come—and they will come—will you stand strong or will your life come crashing down? Anchor your life on the truth by trusting in Jesus Christ and you have help for today and hope for tomorrow. Christianity is typically misunderstood as a religion, something external that we turn to from time to time, when in reality it is a supernatural relationship with the living God. God's presence is within us, so we are never alone, and he will never leave us, so our future is secure when we anchor our lives in him (Deut 31:6; Heb 13:5).

It's important to know we have a strong foundation for life, convinced our beliefs are anchored on the rocks of reality, but this involves digging down deep to see what they're made of. Some people are unwilling to examine life at this level with another person, viewing it as an intensely personal process, but others are open to talk about things that really matter. So when we try to have a conversation that counts, we need to be gentle and respectful, asking the kind of questions that uncover the way people look at the world: "How do you think we got here?" "Why do you think we're here?" "Where do you think we're going?" These kinds of open questions (who, what, where, when, how or why) reveal what people believe about the big picture. Those who distance themselves from belief in God may never have considered the consequences of a world that resulted from random physical forces—that life has no real meaning or absolute value. *Time* magazine once captured the essence of what a godless perspective tells us we can look forward to: "Eventually, [everything] will decay, leaving a featureless, infinitely large void."[2] The logical outcome of this worldview is incompatible with most of the important things about life that stand out and fit together. Meaning and value unashamedly get our attention, and rather than dismiss this fact, we need to look for a worldview that fits them.

The Belief Scale

As we continue this journey, I want to introduce another visual aid that complements the jigsaw guide to making sense of the world and reinforces it. When I was in graduate school, J. P. Moreland used a kind of belief scale to teach how belief works.[3] It is a simple mechanism but its easy application struck a chord with me, to the extent that I still use it when I teach on the subject.

Figure 3.1. The belief scale

Picture an old set of scales, the kind that would tip to the right, tip to the left, or balance in the middle depending on where you place the weight. These positions represent believing that a proposition is true (tipping to the right), believing that a proposition is not true (tipping to the left), or withholding belief about a proposition (balancing in the middle). The weight placed on the scale is reasons to believe one way or the other, and the balance of the scales reflects the balance of belief. (This is similar to the kind of sliding scale used in market research—e.g., "On a scale from one to ten, how strongly do you agree with the following statement?")

The belief scale helps us visualize how reasons tip our beliefs one way or the other, and how rather than switching on or off, our beliefs emerge by degree. This is represented in the diagram using a sliding scale from 1 to 100 percent. A strong belief will be closer to 100 percent and have more (or weightier) reasons to support it; a weak belief will be closer to 1 percent and have fewer (or less weighty) reasons to support it. A decision to withhold belief will reflect the scales sitting at 0 percent because there are no reasons (no weight) to support a belief, or there are equal reasons (and equal weight) on both sides of the scale.

This makes a natural process sound very mechanical, but the truth is we do this every day without thinking about it. Consider my belief that, as I write this, my daughters Sophia and Moriah are at school. This is a strong belief, perhaps as strong as 95 percent, because I have many good reasons to believe it is true. It's a normal school day during school hours, the girls set off as usual this morning, and it's relatively quiet around the house. These reasons have a cumulative effect and result in a strong belief, but it's important to note that it falls short of 100 percent. Why? It's still only an inference to the best explanation, which means it's what I deem most likely to be true based on the information available. Therefore, it is defeatable, which means the belief could hypothetically be defeated by another belief (a defeater) that encourages me to believe otherwise. If this belief is defeated by a defeater, I will have a new belief (whatever belief defeated it), but I still need to leave the door open for a potential defeater defeater. Something out there could still convince me to believe otherwise, and this policy of "leaving the door open" would continue.

Figure 3.2.

The fact that I keep inserting a fallibility clause may surprise some people, particularly when I'm referring to a belief that seems so straightforward. It seems unnecessary and appears to set a dangerous precedent. Indeed it does set a precedent, but it should not unnerve us. Note that despite my humble approach my belief remains strong, and it is not shaken by the fact that I could be wrong. When I have good reason to believe something is true, I will continue to believe it. Others may challenge my belief, suggesting any number of defeaters, but I can fall back on my good reasons to defeat the defeater. I don't have to overcome every objection to survive the ordeal; all I have to do is make sure enough weight is still tipping me in the right direction. It's not easy to upset the scales when they're heavily weighted, and rather than weakening my position, anyone who questions a strong belief will only remind me—and allow me to share—the reason why my belief is so secure. The danger comes when a belief is not reasonably anchored in the real world. A weak belief is vulnerable, which is one reason people would rather not talk about it; if we expose it they may end up believing something else.

Returning to my belief that Sophia and Moriah are at school: it is a strong belief, but every strong belief can get stronger—for example, I could receive a phone call from the girls' school that reassured me they were there. This would bump my belief closer to 100 percent (maybe 99.9 percent), but I still need to leave a little room for the fact I could be mistaken. Perhaps I wonder if Sheryl brought the girls home early as a special surprise, and to heighten the dramatic impact she asked a friend to fake the phone call. The mere suggestion of this alternative would not shake me since it seems unlikely, and it would be unable to outweigh all the good reasons I have to believe the girls are in school. So my belief would remain strong and unmoved.

A strong belief can also get weaker or even go in the opposite direction. If I suddenly thought I heard Sophia and Moriah playing in the house, I would immediately question my belief that they were at school. Take this a step further. If I could see them playing outside my window, my belief would change altogether. It would swing in the opposite direction, and I would now believe that the proposition "Sophia and Moriah are at school" was not true. It would be another strong belief, maybe sitting at negative 99.99 percent on the scale, but I would still have to leave some margin for error. Perhaps a local television program that plays tricks on people has dressed two children to look like my daughters to get my reaction on camera when I think they're absent from school. I (or anyone else) could come up with any number of unlikely scenarios to demonstrate that every belief falls short of absolute certainty. This kind of admission is not fatal; it is not even forceful because—and this is a crucial point—possibility is not synonymous with probability.

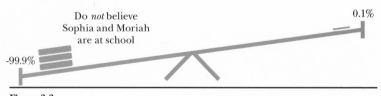

Figure 3.3.

Just because something is possible does not mean it is probable, and something may be possible but entirely improbable. Certainly there are unique times when we believe something that seems entirely improbable, and just because it is improbable does not automatically mean it is not true. But as a general rule our beliefs swing in the direction of probability and good reasons to believe. Take any strong belief you currently hold and reflect on all the good reasons that push you in this direction. Now create a bizarre scenario that highlights the fact that you could be wrong. You (and your belief) will be unmoved by this revelation because it will be like placing a feather on one side of a scale when an elephant already sits on the other side. Strong beliefs are not threatened by mere possibility, and if someone persists in saying, "But you could be wrong," you can agree and then share some of the reasons you believe you are right.

This kind of evaluation is necessary if we are going to share our beliefs in the real world. In the art of pottery, before a pot is released to the public it is fired, which means it is exposed to extremely high temperatures. The heat builds strength and endurance, preparing the object for challenging environments and heated situations. You could say that a pot that's been through the fire has less chance of cracking up. Hopefully you see the comparison. Many people are unwilling to examine the foundation for their beliefs—to put their worldview through the fire, so to speak—and as a result it lacks strength and endurance. They are ill-equipped to handle challenging environments and heated situations, at least not without cracking up. The problem is that Christians are specifically instructed to go into these kinds of situations, and that is why they need to be sure their beliefs have been tried and tested. Opening ourselves to difficult questions can appear to threaten our beliefs, but in reality it strengthens them and prepares us for situations we will face in the real world.

The jigsaw guide overcomes the misunderstanding that we cannot know anything for sure without knowing it all; the fact is we can and do. All our beliefs fall short of absolute certainty, but admitting this prepares us for the day when someone introduces a crack in our belief, and they will. If we engage in conversation and talk about things that really matter, there will be issues we cannot explain and questions we cannot answer. The jigsaw helps prepare us to handle it. Knowing we do not depend on exhaustive knowledge relieves the pressure and prevents our beliefs from shattering into a thousand pieces whenever they are seriously challenged. A strong belief will remain strong despite the fact we could be wrong. J. P. Moreland puts it well:

> Many times we think that believing something with less than complete certainty means we really do not believe it. But this is not true. If you believe something, you must be slightly more certain that it is true than you are that it is false—you must be more than fifty-fifty regarding that belief. And your certainty about that belief can grow.[4]

Someone has said that you do not really hold your beliefs; your beliefs hold you. There is no disputing the fact that a stronger belief makes us more secure. There is a powerful illustration of this in the Bible when Jesus asks a man, "Do you believe I can heal your son?" The man says, "I do believe!" Then he adds, "Help me overcome my unbelief!" (Mk 9:24). Belief and unbelief coexist in this man's mind, and while the presence of the latter does not negate the presence of the former, he knows his belief needs to grow stronger. To accept our beliefs as fallible may shake us, particularly in the short term, but it is the first step toward recovering and securing them for the long-term. Identifying good reasons to believe will tip the scale heavily in the right direction and prepare us for the day difficult questions come—and they will come.

The Myth of Make-Believe

It's exciting to share your beliefs when you have built them on a reasonable foundation because you're confident your worldview resonates with the real world. But what do you say when someone dispassionately responds, "Yeah, well, I can believe what I want." This is the myth of make-believe, something we need to address because the reality is that we cannot believe what we want. Before we do this we must understand that there are things people believe and things people say they believe. The latter may bear no weight and no resemblance to reality, so for the purposes of this discussion we will assume a person's belief actually corresponds to what the person believes to be true.

When someone says, "I can believe what I want," he or she probably feels quite comfortable in this assumption. However, belief lies beyond our direct control. It is influenced by what we think is true, so if we believe that something is not true we cannot simply decide to believe it—even if we say we do. We cannot snap our fingers and make ourselves believe whatever we want. Richard Swinburne has said that "beliefs . . . are always totally involuntary—we do not choose our beliefs; they come to us."[5]

This statement often takes people by surprise, so I enjoy illustrating it by asking a bizarre question: "Do you believe that there's an elephant in the room?" When the audience confirms that there is no elephant on the premises, I tell them to prepare to reconsider. "What if I offered you one million dollars to believe there was an elephant in the room?" I often work with students, so you can be sure this gets their attention—what an incentive to believe! Yet despite the temptation to say whatever it takes to pocket the prize, everyone grasps the nature of the problem.

If you do not believe something to be true, you cannot suddenly make yourself believe it. You can run around and jump up and down, but your belief remains unshaken. Swinburne continues, "Belief is not under our direct voluntary control. . . . I would not be able to just manufacture belief, even in response to the most lucrative inducements. If something seems to me to be the case, I believe it. I can't believe it if it does not seem to me to be the case."[6]

This would be a tragic revelation if it meant we were totally stuck with our beliefs, but thankfully we can indirectly influence them. "While I cannot change my beliefs at an instant, I can set about trying to change them over a period. . . . I can set myself to look for more evidence, knowing that may lead to a change in my beliefs."[7]

So if we are willing to consider good reasons to believe that something is true (either in line with our belief or in opposition to it), we may soon find our belief starting to change. As Steven Davis has said, "To some extent our beliefs are caused by our experiences; and to some extent we can exercise control over the experiences we have. It seems to follow, then, that to some extent our beliefs are under our control."[8] In the same way we can avoid exposing ourselves to something for fear that it could persuade us to believe something we do not want to believe. However, we need to shoot down the myth of make-believe since it suggests that we can simply believe whatever we want. We cannot.

Appeal to Relative Belief

Belief that is grounded in the real world means it is anchored in something outside of ourselves. While our personal experience is a powerful reality and provides many reasons to believe, we need to avoid reducing the truth of the Christian worldview to "It really works for me." We need to build our beliefs on something more than strong emotional attachment, and while we cannot deny the depth of feeling that accompanies Christian belief (indeed this is one of the most wonderful things about it), we need to build a broader base of objective and intellectual support. While all belief is ultimately subjective, subject to the one who believes, it helps to point to things that correspond to the real world and have equal application in the lives of other people.

A story is sometimes told about an atheist who was bold enough to address a large Christian audience in an effort to debunk the credibility of Christian belief. This man was a respected scholar, holding degrees from prestigious universities, and he spoke passionately for more than an hour undermining belief in Jesus Christ. After delivering a powerful presentation, quoting numerous philosophers and theologians, he brought things to a close and sat down, exhausted. The moderator's nervous invitation for questions was met with silence, and members of the partisan audience were clearly uncomfortable, shifting in their seats.

After what seemed like an eternity the silence was broken by the scraping of a chair at the back of the room. Everyone looked to see an old preacher slowly getting to his feet. This man tipped his head to the side, scratched his beard and said, "Well, sir, I thank you for your presentation. I'm afraid I don't have a long list of degrees. I couldn't talk about Greek and Hebrew, like you did. I'm not sure I've heard of the philosophers you mentioned, never mind understand them, but I do have one question."

The crowd's gaze remained fixed, the people eager to hear what the old preacher had to say. They were surprised to see him pick up a small brown paper bag. Looking down, the man reached inside and pulled out a shiny red apple. After taking a big bite, he returned his attention to the speaker. "Just one question, sir, about this apple. Does it taste bitter or does it taste sweet?"

The atheist looked confused as he stood up and slowly returned to the microphone. Slightly hesitating, he responded, "Well, sir, I'm sure I don't know . . . because I haven't tasted your apple."

The old preacher grinned and with a twinkle in his eye said, "That's right, and you haven't tasted my Jesus!" As he slowly sat down, the man next to him stood up and started clapping. He was followed by another, and another, until the whole room was standing and cheering. The atheist, unnerved and unable to respond, gathered his papers together and left the room.

I once shared this story during a class I was teaching at a local church, and it was interesting to see people's reactions. There were smiles all around until I introduced a twist in my presentation to prove an important point. The room grew quiet when I said that despite my sympathies for the warm feelings people were experiencing, this story is actually a powerful illustration of what we should not do when it comes to sharing and defending our Christian beliefs. In fact, we do the gospel a disservice when we claim that Christianity is true because "it tastes good to me." When this pragmatic view is the basis of our belief (and our sole recommendation to others), pity the person who decides it does not taste good to them. They find themselves on the outside, with no way in and through no fault of their own. We don't choose what tastes good to us. Generally we find ourselves liking something, loathing it or being apathetic about it. If taste is all we have to go on, some will have good reason not to believe the Christian worldview, and at that point there is nothing more to say.

For the record, Christianity does taste sweet to me (and to every Christian) in a number of ways, but it can also lead to difficult situations and bitter experiences. A strong Christian once said to me, "I don't like telling people, 'God loves you and has a wonderful plan for your life,' because part of God's plan for you could be to suffer in order to bring him greater glory." Read some of the amazing accounts of Christians who have suffered terribly for the Christian faith and you marvel at the way they still experience God's joy and peace. Christianity does not promise that life will be a bed of roses; it actually says the opposite is likely (Jn 16:33). But it does claim to be true, which means it is true for everyone.

Christianity should resonate with people because it resonates with reality. Atheists may try to undermine it, quoting various philosophers and theologians, but we do not have to wobble weakly on the other side of the table. Many of the greatest minds in history have been firm defenders of the Christian faith, sharing good reasons to believe it is true. The responsibility to stand up for the reasonable foundation of Christianity is ours in every discussion about truth, belief, faith and doubt. Reason always falls short of persuading others to accept or embrace the truth and teaching of Jesus Christ, but it powerfully anchors belief in the real world. It also distances Christianity from the relative appeal of what tastes good to me. Relying on our feelings offers no real security, and it is easy to privatize a belief when it appears fragile. Christian belief that lacks reasonable support is often withdrawn from public conversation so that it can be preserved and protected.

There is no shame in having a strong emotional tie to a deeply held belief. Indeed it would be sad if we lacked the God-given feelings we were created to enjoy. But we need to secure our beliefs on a firmer foundation. It is difficult to share a feeling-based belief with people who feel differently. For example, if we argue that the Bible is worth reading because it makes me feel good, we may draw a quick rebuttal from someone who says she read it, got bored with it and gave up on it. (In fact, those who read the Bible and feel bad may be closer to understanding it.)

Religions and cults that lack a reasonable foundation often default to the realm of relative belief. One day two Mormon evangelists came to my door. We enjoyed a good discussion, although there was no doubt that we completely disagreed about our respective solutions to the problem of the human condition. However, we did seem to agree on the spiraling moral decay in society, and I suggested that a large part of the problem was a tendency to use feelings to establish the right thing to do. The two young men nodded their approval, but in spite of this they left me with the Book of Mormon and this challenge: "We invite all men everywhere to read the Book of Mormon, to ponder in their hearts the message it contains, and then to ask God, the Eternal Father, in the name of Christ if the book is true. Those who pursue this course and ask in faith will gain a testimony of its truth and divinity by the power of the Holy Ghost."[9]

Mormons often present this challenge as a means of proving that Mormonism is true, and they claim that all you have to do is read this passage and watch for a subsequent sensation: a "burning in the bosom." This is allegedly how God supernaturally confirms the truth of Mormonism. I was not moved or motivated by the Mormon challenge, and the test fails for three main reasons.

First, it is circular. You need to believe the Book of Mormon to believe that this is the test for truth for the Book of Mormon. If you already believe the Book of Mormon you do not need to take the test and pray the prayer. If you do not believe the Book of Mormon you will not believe this is a valid test for truth for the Book of Mormon, so there is no point taking the test and praying the prayer. Either way Christians can respond with a polite "thank you, but no thank you."

The second reason is based on the biblical injunction to critically question the source of every alleged supernatural communication or revelation. Paul wrote in the New Testament, "Even if we or an angel from heaven should preach a gospel other than the one we preached to you, let him be eternally condemned" (Gal 1:8). This passage highlights the danger of angelic deception and specifically ties in with the origin of Mormonism, where supposedly an angel appeared to Joseph Smith and preached another gospel. Paul also wrote about the difficulty of relying on the warmth of our immediate experience to discern right and wrong since "Satan himself masquerades as an angel of light" (2 Cor 11:14).

The third reason is the danger of defaulting to feelings to determine right and wrong, which brings us back to the problem of those who say everything is relative. In my conversation with the Mormons they agreed that this kind of approach was responsible for making wrong moral decisions, but then (without realizing it) they suggested I make a similar mistake to establish the truth of their religion.[10] Feelings should never be used as the lone arbiter of truth—about morality or Mormonism—and while the irony of this was obvious to me it seemed less obvious to them.

Anchoring your faith in your feelings can make you feel good and is convenient since it takes no time or effort on our part, but it does not match up to the authority of the Bible or the teaching of Jesus Christ. Our capacity to feel is God-given and wonderful, but feelings are vulnerable, and God told us to engage our minds in the process of discovering the truth to help keep our feelings in check (Mt 22:37; 1 Thess 5:21).

Evidence That Encourages Belief

Christians can rejoice in the way beliefs impact our feelings, as well as the way our feelings impact our beliefs, and we should be prepared to experience God at work in every area of our lives. But Jesus was clear about what holds everything together. He said, "I am the way and the truth and the life" (Jn 14:6-7). We cannot afford to build our belief solely on the way we feel at any given moment. Instead we must stand on the conviction of our hearts, minds and souls that we know the truth. C. S. Lewis relayed a crucial step on the road to his conversion in these terms:

> You must picture me alone in that room in Magdalene [College], night after night, feeling, whenever my mind lifted even a second from my work, the steady, unrelenting approach of Him whom I so earnestly desired not to meet. . . . I gave in, and admitted that God was God, and knelt and prayed: perhaps, that night, the most dejected and reluctant convert in all England.[11]

Lewis later made the decision to commit his life to Jesus Christ, and it was not all doom and gloom. In fact, his autobiography is called *Surprised by Joy*. But his belief was the result of supernatural compulsion and reasonable conviction that Christianity was true—the joy came later. Lewis experienced the inner work of the Holy Spirit, but he was also challenged by the intelligibility of the Christian message and the depth of Christian thinkers, such as G. K. Chesterton, George MacDonald and J. R. R. Tolkien. God has provided good reasons to believe that the Christian worldview is true, and he will often use a reasonable presentation of the gospel as part of the process to draw people closer to him.

The Bible contains many powerful examples of how reason bolsters our faith and encourages us to share with others (see Acts 17), but I often turn to a very simple example given by Luke in the introduction to his Gospel: "Since I myself have carefully investigated everything from the beginning, it seemed good also to me to write an orderly account . . . so that you may know the certainty of the things you have been taught" (Lk 1:3-4). Luke prefaced his Gospel of the life, death, resurrection and ascension of Jesus Christ by reminding us of the importance of a reasonable foundation for Christian belief, and he went on to provide a solid platform for knowing the truth.

Something to Think About

I once spoke at a student conference on ethical issues, and I was open about the fact that my position on a particular subject was anchored in the Christian worldview. Sheryl came with me, and later she had the privilege of observing one of the student discussion groups. She told me one girl was deeply troubled, telling the group, "I agree with what he was saying, but I'm not a Christian." This student recognized that a particular belief seemed true and it stood out in the world, but she was confused because she did not share my worldview. There was conflict between what she believed about life and what she assumed to be true about the big picture, and suddenly she had a lot to think about.

People need to be given the opportunity to stand back and consider how they see the world and whether it really makes sense of life's broken pieces. Be prepared to initiate this kind of discussion by asking the question "How does your worldview help you make sense of the world?" It's a difficult question that taps into sensitive issues, and it can be deeply troubling when someone begins to understand that their outlook on life is not rooted in reality. But this can open the door to meaningful dialogue. For our part, we need to know why the Christian worldview is the fusion of reason and revelation that resonates with reality. When we do we will discover the confidence to ask this question and have the conversation.

Summary
We need to be ready to burst the bubble of those who think we should be left alone to believe what we want and then encourage them to build their belief on the rocks of reality. All beliefs are not created equal, you can be sure without being (absolutely) certain, and powerful reasons to believe the Christian worldview is true can tip people in the right direction.

Discussion
How would you normally share your beliefs? How could this chapter help you be more effective?

What are some common obstacles to talking openly about your beliefs? What have you learned that will help you overcome them?

Recommended Reading
J. P. Moreland. *Love Your God with All Your Mind.* Colorado Springs: NavPress, 1997.

Timothy Keller. *The Reason for God.* London: Hodder and Stoughton, 2008.

4

FAITH

Be Prepared to Anchor It

"So you're a Christian, a person of faith!
I could never live like that."

"Live like what?"

"Live by faith! I need good reasons to believe something.
You know—evidence."

"I do know what you mean, but what makes you think
Christianity isn't reasonable?"

"It's religion—a blind leap of faith—
something out of touch with the real world."

"Reasonable faith" can sound like an oxymoron in light of
the religious caricatures that fill our popular media, particularly
when it comes to faith in a Christian context. It's common to
depict people of faith as decidedly dippy—it would seem that
you're either a reasonable person who puts her life together with
the nuts and bolts of the real world or a person of faith who disen-
gages his mind and lives with his head stuck in the clouds. Such a

lazy misrepresentation flies in the face of history; many of the greatest thinkers have been Christians who anchored their religious faith on a reasonable foundation.[1] But cultural forces seem dedicated to perpetuating the myth and deepening the divide.

Among the contemporary examples of this great divorce, solidifying the idea that faith and reason are like oil and water, is a powerful scene from the movie *Indiana Jones and the Last Crusade*. It is a wonderful action-adventure story with Indiana Jones the swashbuckling archaeologist in pursuit of the Holy Grail. As the plot reaches its climax, Indiana must overcome three distinctly "religious" challenges to realize his goal and reach the relic. We will focus on the final test since it creates a lasting impression of what it means to be a person of faith.

Indiana has successfully completed the first two challenges, but his journey comes to an abrupt halt when he arrives at the edge of a yawning chasm. The path toward the Grail is still visible on the other side, and our hero remembers the essence of this obstacle—to leap and prove your worth—but there is a problem: it would be impossible to jump this distance. To add to the suspense, the screams of Indiana's father remind us that his life is hanging in the balance, and what began as a historical quest has been transformed into a journey of hope. The legendary healing powers of the Grail are the only thing that can save his father's life, so Indiana prepares to do whatever it takes to overpower his (common) senses, muttering the mantra "It's a leap of faith!"

What happens next is a significant gesture in this context. He briefly closes his eyes, and then Indiana Jones, the brilliant archaeologist who normally keeps his philosophical feet on the ground, chooses to step out into thin air. It is a dramatic moment, enough to make the audience hold its collective breath, and to the surprise of everyone his foot lands on something solid. The camera swings to the side, offering a different perspective, and we see there was a bridge there after all. Previously camouflaged against the rocks, it was invisible to the naked eye, and a blind leap of faith was required for Indiana to prove his worth and pass the test.

The object lesson? Religious faith is choosing to believe when there is no good reason to do so. In fact, the movie stretches this further: you choose to believe when there is every reason not to do so. When everything you hold true about the world screams, "Don't believe it!" you choose to believe it anyway because you are a person of faith. The movie makes this seem admirable, but to believe under these conditions in the real world does not make sense—because it's nonsense.

Imagine you adopted this approach and applied it consistently in your life: "I will believe when there is no reason to do so and every reason not to do so." How long would you survive? You certainly could not get out of serious trouble; you could not even get out of bed in the morning. This topsy-turvy approach reflects Hollywood's fuzzy depiction of religious faith, but it's not the real faith of real people in the real world. When "people of faith" are portrayed this way, it's no surprise to see them treated with either sympathy or disdain. We need to clear up this kind of confusion about biblical faith and restore it to its rightful place, anchoring it on a reasonable foundation.

Faith Defined

Opening the pages of a dictionary will not necessarily help us re-capture the true meaning of a word because dictionaries are, to a certain extent, at the mercy of linguistic trends. Instead of preserving a particular definition they must be flexible enough to encompass the fluctuations of language and reflect the vernacular. What means one thing today may mean something different tomorrow.

Look up the word *faith* in the *Oxford English Dictionary* and among the denotations you will find a popular description: "strong belief in the doctrines of a religion based on spiritual conviction rather than proof." The suggestion is that faith is an irrational belief, a view popularized by Bertrand Russell when he said, "We may define 'faith' as the firm belief in something for which there is no evidence."[2] And Russell is not the only one who holds this definition.

It may come as a surprise to hear Christians describe their faith as something completely distinct from reason, or even in opposition to it, but it happens often. I once spoke on the importance of reasonable faith at a Christian event where one man became visibly upset. He argued that our intellect was totally corrupted by sin and we needed to reject reason and rely on God's Word by faith alone. While it's difficult to reason with someone who rejects our ability to reason, since anything I say could instantly be dismissed as unreasonable, it's worth pointing out this argument collapses on itself.

If this man is right and our intellect is totally corrupted by sin, then he cannot reasonably make this argument since his intellect is corrupted too, and his conclusion should be rejected. If he is wrong and our intellect is not totally corrupted by sin, then his argument (that it is corrupted) is also wrong, and once again his conclusion should be rejected. Either way his conclusion should be rejected because we cannot reasonably deny reason without affirming it at the same time. We need to share these things clearly but respectfully, and our goal should always be to build others up in the truth, not tear them down. God has given us the power of reason to bolster our faith and help us connect with the real world, and we need to be prepared to stand up for it and defend it.

Many Christians who make the case for blind biblical faith point to particular passages, such as Jesus' words in John's Gospel: "Blessed are those who have not seen and yet have believed" (Jn 20:29). Jesus' words are directed to Thomas, the disciple who lacked the faith to believe that he was risen from the dead without visible proof. Jesus was commending those who believed he was alive without seeing him resurrected, but that did not mean they did not have reason to place their faith in him. The New Testament is full of wonderful reasons for people then and now to place their faith in the risen Christ—fulfilled prophecy, powerful miracles and the transformed lives of the disciples. All are evidences that fuel the fire of faith, and the Gospels were written as reasonable accounts of the life, death, resurrection and ascension of Jesus Christ to encourage faith in him (Jn 20:30).

The Bible is clear that it takes faith to trust in Jesus Christ—a faith that is supernaturally stirred and that fills in the gaps where reason falls short. But that does not mean reason is absent from the process. Some people like to quote eleventh-century church father St. Anselm's "faith seeking understanding," suggesting that blind faith comes first and reasonable understanding comes later. However, Anselm also said, "If anyone does not know . . . things that we must believe about God or his creation, I think he could at least convince himself of most of these things by reason alone, if he is even moderately intelligent."[3] This reflection reminds us that reason can draw us closer to Christian faith. We don't know it all, but we can know enough to encourage faith and secure it on a reasonable foundation. There are many things about this world that lie beyond our comprehension, which is no surprise since we're trying to understand the mind of God. Yet we need to remember that the Bible consistently describes a Christian faith that is wedded to reason, and we cannot afford to break up this relationship.

There is no biblical injunction against the use of our critical faculties. In fact, Jesus said the opposite: "Love the Lord your God with all your heart and with all your soul and with all your mind" (Mt 22:37). The Bible teaches that human beings were created by God with the capacity to reason, and this God-given gift enables us to draw closer to him. As Ravi Zacharias says, "God has put enough into the world to make faith in him a most reasonable thing, and he has left enough out to make it impossible to live by sheer reason or observation alone."[4] Every aspect of human personality is damaged by sin, but we are still required to love God with all our hearts (although inadequately), with all our souls (albeit insufficiently) and with all our minds (admittedly incompletely). To suggest that we cannot engage our minds in the journey of faith because it is damaged by sin would require, for the sake of consistency, that we refrain from engaging our emotions too. Our feelings have not survived the fall unscathed, yet many who demote the role of reason ignore the impact of sin on our feelings. This is just as troubling as those at the other end of the spectrum who dismiss the fragility of our emotions and elevate the mind. The Bible is clear that we need to use both to anchor our faith and grow in our walk with God.

We cannot leave this subject without turning to a popular verse that is often used to defend a blind approach to biblical faith. In the book of Hebrews, the eleventh chapter opens with stirring words: "Now faith is being sure of what we hope for and certain of what we do not see" (Heb 11:1). This verse in isolation would seem to support that biblical faith is blind; however, taking a verse in isolation often means taking a verse out of context, so we need to stand back and see this verse as part of the bigger picture.

The book of Hebrews celebrates the great heroes of the faith, those commended by God because they believed yet "none of them received what had been promised" (Heb 11:39). The Greek word translated "faith" here is *pistis*, which means trusting and believing, but there is no sense that this word is ever used to represent a blind commitment. In fact, Luke uses the same word in Acts 17:31 when he records Paul's famous "Men of Athens" address; here the word is generally translated "proof." Paul is referring to Christ's visible resurrection as proof or reason to have faith (*pistis*) in his divine nature, so the point is that biblical faith is reasonable. You do not close your eyes to have faith in Jesus Christ—you open them.

Hebrews strengthens this argument when we pause and ponder the lives of those being elevated and celebrated. Consider Abel. He was a man of faith who sincerely trusted in God (in contrast to his brother Cain), but imagine how his faith was forged. If your father was Adam, the first human being, directly created by God, what captivating accounts would you have heard growing up and bouncing on his knee? Next is Enoch, a man whose faith flowed from the fact he "walked with God" and enjoyed such a close relationship that he never died but was taken directly into God's presence. Then there is Noah, grandson of Methuselah, the oldest man in the Bible, who lived for nearly a thousand years. No doubt his faith was steeled by circumstances and quickened when God spoke directly to him. Os Guinness has underlined the fact that "Abraham's faith was not the least blind. Quite the contrary. It is precisely because Abraham knew God that he could trust God in the dark."[5] These great men of faith did not see all that God had promised—that much is true. But what they did see gave them great confidence (and faith) in what was unseen.

Regardless of where people stand on these details (some refuse to take the Bible so literally), the point is that the biblical definition of faith is not "believing when there is no reason." Instead, God has provided an abundance of reasons to have faith in him. Jesus himself invited those who were tempted to be skeptical about his true identity to reflect on the evidence: the blind are seeing, the lame are walking, the deaf are hearing (Mt 11:2-5). Trusting in God, like trusting anything, always requires a step of faith. But rather than closing your eyes and stumbling in the darkness, biblical faith is keeping your eyes open and walking in the light (Ps 119:105).

Faith Without God
It is important to respond to Christians who unknowingly undermine biblical faith by characterizing it as blind, and while many do it for the right reasons (realizing the problem of leaning on our own understanding), we need to encourage a more balanced approach that takes into account God's provision of a beautiful mind. However, the greater (and more critical) work is re-

sponding to those whose *raison d'être* is to destroy the reasonable foundation for religious faith, a movement that has gained momentum with the rise of the New Atheism. As Phillip Johnson has said, "One of the most important stereotypes in naturalistic thinking is that 'religion' is based on faith rather than reason, and that persons who believe in God are inherently unwilling to follow the truth wherever it may lead because that path leads to Naturalism."[6] Among those proud to beat this drum is Richard Dawkins. In *The God Delusion* he makes his position clear: "The whole point of religious faith, its strength and chief glory, is that it does not depend on rational justification. The rest of us are expected to defend our prejudices. But ask a religious person to justify their faith and you infringe 'religious liberty.'"[7]

Dawkins deliberately drives a wedge between faith and reason, suggesting that religion follows faith and science follows reason, but it is interesting to note that these are the philosophical musings of a "scientist." Dawkins is stepping outside the boundaries of his own discipline, subtly removing his lab coat and trying to squeeze into a tweed jacket, and while he is free to muse as much as the next person, we need to appreciate that he is not speaking *ex cathedra*. Indeed, when the suit does not fit one should not wear it. Atheism does not set us free and provide answers to life's most difficult questions; it leads us into greater bondage and confusion. In the preface of his book, Dawkins makes this opening statement:

> As a child, my wife hated her school and wished she could leave. Years later, when she was in her twenties, she disclosed this unhappy fact to her parents, and her mother was aghast: "But darling, why didn't you come to us and tell us?" Lalla's reply is my text for today: "But I didn't know I could."[8]

Dawkins steps into his pulpit and tries to draw a parallel, suggesting that many people are unhappily schooled in religion and left feeling like they are stuck with nowhere else to go. Dawkins's

motives, therefore, appear benevolent, helping set people free and
introducing them to the rational alternative, atheism. It is ironic
that Dawkins chooses to base his premise for writing the book on
human freedom, since this is one of the primary reasons his
work—and his worldview—come crashing down.

To begin to shed light on this and steer Dawkins back on the
right path, I would like to turn to an unlikely source: talented
actor, comedian and outspoken atheist Ricky Gervais. In 2011
Gervais was invited to host the Golden Globes, one of Hollywood's
premier award ceremonies broadcast around the world. Gervais
got people's attention when he closed the evening's entertainment
by announcing, "And thank you to God for making me an atheist!"
It was a curious remark considering the context, but he has said
this kind of thing more than once.[9] Apparently Gervais wanted to
use this platform to make an important point: if God exists—and
is in control of everything—then the fact that Ricky Gervais is an
atheist is not really Ricky Gervais's fault. It is God's fault. Maybe
Gervais wanted to defend himself in case God was watching.

There is a lot about Ricky Gervais I like. He's a great communi-
cator and demonstrates true insight into human nature and
popular culture, and he has the courage to raise important issues
and ask difficult questions. However, his reasoning about belief
and freedom in this instance is the wrong way round—and needs
to be put right. If God exists, at least the God of the Bible, then
God is all-powerful, but he also chose to create people with free
will.[10] This means that each of us has been granted freedom: to
affirm belief in God or to reject belief in God. If Ricky Gervais
chooses to describe himself as an atheist, then this is ultimately
up to him. We have already highlighted the way beliefs seem to
well up within us, involuntarily and influenced by reasons (one
way or another), but we can still choose to accept the belief or
reject it. Gervais could be stirred by the tremendous order, beauty
and complexity in the world—and in ourselves—only to shrug his

shoulders and shake his head. Ironically, Ricky Gervais is free from responsibility only if atheism (or naturalism) is true. One of the most powerful and swept-under-the-carpet consequences of atheism is determinism: there is no free will. Richard Dawkins demonstrates this:

> In a universe of blind physical forces and genetic replication, some people are going to get hurt, other people are going to get lucky, and you won't find any rhyme or reason in it, nor any justice. The universe we observe has precisely the properties we should expect if there is, at bottom, no design, no purpose, no evil and no good, nothing but blind, pitiless indifference. . . . DNA neither knows nor cares. DNA just is. And we dance to its music.[11]

According to this worldview human beings are just a bunch of physical stuff programmed to act a certain way, dancing to our DNA. We are basically determined by two things: nature and nurture. Nature refers to our genes and nurture our environment. These provide a series of inputs—pushing our buttons—and whatever they add up to comes out in our behavior. We have no control because there is no "us," no ghost in the machine,[12] and there is no basis in this worldview for suggesting that free will suddenly squirts into existence.[13] Ricky Gervais is only dancing to the music of his DNA and needs to come up with a new catchphrase: "Thank you, atheism, for making me an atheist!"

More than one person has written in response to Dawkins's *The God Delusion*, pointing out the delusions of atheism in general and of Dawkins in particular.[14] If atheism is true we do not have the freedom to reject religion. We do not have the freedom to do anything. Faith in God is something we find ourselves having or not having, and whatever faith we end up with, there is no reason to believe that one is better than another since there is no objective moral standard to judge them—which is another fatal flaw of naturalistic atheism.

I once had an opportunity to go to dinner with a group of atheists after a debate. It was a lively discussion, and while a number of issues came up, two left a lasting impression. The first was the reaction of one member of the group when I told him I was a Christian because I was committed to knowing the truth. I explained that I would reject Christianity if I truly believed it were false and that my faith was secured on many good reasons to believe that it was true—both evidential and existential. My dinner companion seemed never to have heard anything beyond "personal testimony," so I shared some powerful reasons to believe in the resurrection of Jesus Christ, based on the credibility of the biblical text.[15] The second memorable moment came when I asked the atheists a question: how do you deal with the fact that according to your worldview there is no free will? One person said he was willing to accept that this was true, but he was immediately refuted by the others. While they could not offer an explanation for the source of free will, they were unwilling to deny the reality of our experience. I smiled as I sat back and watched them continue to debate the matter among themselves.

Many atheists, Dawkins and Gervais included, like to smuggle the benefits of a Christian perspective into their own worldview, and the belief in free will is one of the primary interlopers. Dawkins uses this freedom to attack religion in general and Christianity in particular, which is a bit like tearing off someone else's arm and then beating him with it. However, when we learn to anticipate this we can do something about it. If you find yourself in this situation, draw attention to the fact that if we are all just a collection of chemicals, then we will say and do whatever chemistry determines. There is no real "me" or "you" who can choose what to do or not to do, and atheists who try to defend free will only undermine their position and strengthen the case and credibility of the Christian worldview.

These kinds of shoot-yourself-in-the-foot assumptions are one reason Dawkins is taken less seriously among more stringent scientists and philosophers (not to mention their dislike for his invective). Michael Ruse, a philosopher from England who has a winsome style and regularly contributes to the science-versus-religion debate, says, "Unlike the new atheists, I take scholarship seriously. I have written that *The God Delusion* made me ashamed to be an atheist and I meant it."[16] Anthony Flew, who was one of the foremost defenders of atheism in the latter part of the twentieth century, calls Dawkins "a secularist bigot."[17] However, while Dawkins may lack credibility in serious circles, his sound bites and straw men are tailor-made for popular culture, so we cannot afford to ignore him. In fact, in one sense I would argue that Christians should thank God for him.

One of the most difficult obstacles to sharing the Christian worldview is having the opportunity to talk about things that really matter, and outspoken atheism is always preferable to dull disinterest. Os Guinness has said, "Rebellion against God does not begin with the clenched fist of atheism but with the self-satisfied heart of the one for whom 'thank you' is redundant."[18] In other words, the greatest challenge to Christianity is not antipathy but apathy. Christians should get excited when they encounter a passionate atheist—this is a person who cares. Take the opportunity to ask how his or her worldview came about and what supports it. Sit me down on a plane next to an outspoken atheist and I will look forward to a vibrant conversation. Sit me down next to someone who shrugs her shoulders about life and says, "Whatever!" and my soul sinks because there is nothing meaningful left to say.

Whenever you hear someone say the choice is between faith and reason, or the dividing line is between religion and science, you know that atheism has left its mark and done its work. Let me add that while I appreciate Dawkins's raising such important issues, I do not celebrate the fact he thumbs his nose in the direction of God. This position—and decision—has dire and eternal consequences, and I genuinely hope and pray that one day he will see the light and embrace the truth. Yet I want to underline how God can take anyone (or anything) dedicated to undermining the truth of Christianity and use it to strengthen the credibility of the gospel, even providing greater opportunities to share it.

When you hear something that suggests, "Faith is believing what you know ain't true,"[19] there are basically two ways to redress the balance and restore clarity to the conversation. First, educate people about the reasonable component of religion. Second, enlighten people on the faith-based component of science. As Chesterton noted, "It is idle to talk always of the alternative of reason and faith. Reason itself is a matter of faith. It is an act of faith to assert that our thoughts have any relation to reality at all."[20]

Dawkins creates a false dichotomy between faith and reason, suggesting that faith is flighty, and he visibly recoils if anyone dares suggest that he is a person of faith. He pretends to distance himself from all faith-based belief, suggesting that it is completely irrational, and we need to point out the fundamental flaws in this approach. William Lane Craig is a Christian philosopher who regularly accomplishes this with razor-like logic, and in a debate with Peter Atkins he did so memorably. Atkins is an atheist and was a professor of chemistry at Oxford University when he confidently challenged Craig to state something that science could not prove. Craig was clearly delighted at the opportunity and rattled off his top five:

1. Logical and mathematical truths: Science cannot prove them because it presupposes them.

2. Metaphysical truths: For example, there are minds that exist other than my own, or the external world is real.

3. Ethical beliefs: You can't show by science whether the Nazi scientists in the camps did anything evil.

4. Aesthetic judgments: The beautiful, like the good, cannot be scientifically proven.

5. Science itself: You need to make certain assumptions in order to do science—for example, assuming that things in the present resemble things in the past and will resemble things in the future.[21]

Craig has said that "reason's role is that of a servant. Reason is a God-given instrument to help us better understand and defend our faith."[22] We cannot even begin to conduct scientific inquiry without having faith in the scientific method—science has to assume there is regularity in nature and that the external world is real. The scientific method helps us interact with the world in a wonderful way, but scientists have to assume that certain things are true by faith. On this basis Atkins and Dawkins are, like the rest of us, people of faith, and it is important to keep them humble by reminding them. Be prepared to scratch the surface of an atheist's belief, but beware—many atheists do not like being scratched.

As if this were not humbling enough for Dawkins and company, there is another crucial fact to expose when it comes to atheism (either old or new)—the blind belief that rational human beings have emerged from a nonrational world. In chapter one we considered how philosopher John Gray, a self-described religious skeptic (a title that seems to grant him some degree of critical immunity), has powerfully unmasked the more outspoken atheist by stating that "humans cannot be other than irrational. Curiously, this is a conclusion few rationalists have been ready to accept."[23]

If it's true that as Bertrand Russell states we are ultimately the accidental outcome of a collocation of atoms, the rationality of atheism will implode under cross-examination. C. S. Lewis said, "A strict materialism refutes itself for the reasons given long ago by Professor Haldane: 'If my mental processes are determined wholly by the motions of atoms in my brain, I have no reason to suppose that my beliefs are true . . . and hence I have no reason for supposing my brain to be composed of atoms.'"[24] Unfortunately, this means there is no scientific basis for believing that human beings are rationally equipped to do science, and when "people of science" try to distance themselves from "people of faith," we need to be ready to bring them back down to earth—often with a bump. As John Polkinghorne has said, "The scientist and the theologian both work by faith, a realist trust in the rational reliability of our understanding of experience."[25]

Faith and Feeling

When faith comes under attack it often seeks refuge in the realm of feeling, and when it goes in this direction many people are quick to follow. There is something comforting about keeping things close to your chest—and close to your heart—and we've already described this temptation in the context of truth and belief. If my faith is anchored in feelings then it is protected since you cannot criticize it, and when it is based on my feelings it should be respected since everyone can have their own faith their own way.

Some religions encourage this kind of unquestioning approach to faith. Many Eastern worldviews begin with the directive to stop thinking and empty your mind: "When your mind is without anything and you are no-minds, then you are free and spiritual, empty and marvelous."[26] Biblical Christianity stands in opposition to this. It encourages us to enjoy the feelings God provides and then use our minds to build our faith. This component is one reason Christianity has been scrutinized for centuries—often by those with a direct agenda to undermine it. However, the Bible stands strong: a regular bestseller, it enjoys critical support from many scholars today.[27]

Contrast this critical approach with Islam and the Qur'an, where you cannot speak a word against it without triggering a barrage of abuse—even personal threats. I have met many warm and wonderful Muslims, and I am not suggesting that Islam should be considered an unthinking faith driven by feeling. The Muslim worldview has been supported by great minds and deep thinkers. However, you have to question the level of debate in a society where only one side has the freedom to speak—and the freedom to think.

Reason is woven into every aspect of making sense of the world, and faith based on feelings alone loses its attraction when we try to put it into practice. Imagine that my family embraces a faith based entirely on our feelings. As a result when my son, Asher, is old enough to cross the road I will walk him to the edge of the pavement, tell him to close his eyes, and encourage him to listen to his heart to decide if it is safe to cross. I may be aware that other parents encourage their children to stop, look and listen, but I dismiss this as too old-fashioned. The listen-to-your-heart crossing code is our preference. What kind of support would this approach receive in our community? Local schools would not introduce it into their curriculum as part of a move to embrace diversity because it is dangerous and out of touch with reality. Anyone who cared for my family could not happily stand back and leave us alone; they would be moved to try and reason with me—before it was too late.

Perhaps this example seems extreme, but think about it for a moment. How many relationships fall apart because one person decided to close his or her mind and do what felt good at the time? Think of the lives that lie in tatters because a desire for instant satisfaction overruled a deeper sense of responsibility. Maybe we do not employ this approach all the time, but once can be more than enough. One man who seems to have embraced this philosophy—in every area of his life—is named Vissarion. A former Russian traffic policeman, he hit the headlines a few years ago when, apparently, he claimed to be the incarnated Christ, the anointed one of God. Styling himself on the blue-eyed icon popularized in nineteenth-century Europe, Vissarion has drawn thousands of followers to Siberia to live near him and worship him. His interviews reveal an increasing reluctance to say too much about his teaching and true identity, but his faith was borne out of the conscious decision to reject reason and rely solely on his feelings. Perhaps unsurprisingly, the faith of his followers takes a similar trajectory.[28]

Vissarion offers no reasonable basis for people to follow him or his teaching. He depends heavily on the feeling he generates within himself and in those around him. Followers claim to experience something special when they meet him, and many say they feel that he is the reincarnated Jesus Christ. Detaching our faith from reality in this way makes us extremely vulnerable. God created our capacity for emotion, and feelings can be wonderful, but they are not a reliable way to discover what is true about the world. In fact, relying on feelings alone is one of the best ways to stop people from discovering the truth. C. S. Lewis spoke of the danger of closing your mind to reason in the context of seeking the truth about God: "If you do not listen to theology, that will not mean that you have no ideas about God. It will mean you have a lot of wrong ones."[29]

God has given us minds with the capacity for reason, and we must employ this in our search for truth. Religious faiths designed to lead us away from truth will do whatever they can to stop us from using the mind God gave us. Abandonment of reason is the surest way to fall into deception. Even though the Bible presents a reasonable approach to growing our faith, this goes against the grain of a culture that promotes the heart at the expense of the head, and sometimes Christians fall into the trap. We can admit that our ability to reason is limited, damaged and often overruled by selfish motives, but reason remains an integral part of the process of faith-building. We need to be prepared to use it, share it and defend it.

Faith and Reason

C. S. Lewis famously quipped, "Faith . . . is the art of holding on to things your reason has once accepted, in spite of your changing moods."[30] When faith rests solely on a powerful experience of

God we may struggle to maintain it when the memory fades, and if our faith depends only on a time when we heard God speak, we may be shaken when he seems silent.[31] One woman expressed an interest in the ministry of Reason Why because she wanted to reinforce her faith. She had been a Christian for a long time and had come to Christ as a result of a powerful experience. Her concern? The memory of that wonderful day was starting to fade. Os Guinness has warned us of this danger: "If there is 'no reason why' when faith is present, there will be 'no reason why not' when doubt arrives."[32] Powerful experiences of God are deeply meaningful, but we need to prepare for leaner times by securing our faith on a firm foundation. As Ravi Zacharias observes, "None of us lives comfortably with a vacuous faith. There ought to be both substance to our faith and an object of our faith."[33]

Engaging our minds and establishing reasonable faith helps us deal with difficult days and difficult questions, just as disengaging our minds and the lack of reasonable support can weaken our faith and cause it to crumble. Faith in God is not walking in the dark, it is walking in the light. Jesus said, "I am the light of the world" (Jn 8:12), and he came to reveal the truth so we could live in light of God's revelation. The reality of God is visible in the natural world because "the heavens declare the glory of God; the skies proclaim the work of his hands. Day after day they pour forth speech; night after night they display knowledge. There is no speech or language where their voice is not heard" (Ps 19:1-3). What is clearly stated in the Old Testament is echoed in the New Testament: "For since the creation of the world God's invisible qualities—his eternal power and divine nature—have been clearly seen, being understood from what has been made, so that men are without excuse" (Rom 1:20).

Faith is necessary when it comes to trusting God about the big picture because we will never completely know or understand, but God has provided an enormous number of important pieces of the puzzle that fit together. Faith is required wherever knowledge falls short, and knowledge will always fall short, but biblical faith is built on solid ground. Christian faith is a reasonable faith—whether or not people choose to accept those reasons and believe. There is wisdom in this world that can lead us to God, but there is also wisdom in this world that will lead us away from God. That's why the apostle Paul tells us to "take captive every thought to make it obedient to Christ" (2 Cor 10:5) and every Christian is called to "be transformed by the renewing of your mind" (Rom 12:2)—so we can understand more of the mind of God and resist the influence of the world when it pulls us in another direction.

The importance of leaning on God's Word to help us discern truth from error is pivotal in Paul's teaching, and the book of Acts reveals that he was not above being judged by the same standard. Although Paul's teaching was difficult for its original hearers to comprehend (see 2 Pet 3:16), the stature of his ministry could have resulted in people resorting to blind acceptance. The Bereans refused to do this, carefully weighing everything to make sure it was in line with the Scriptures (Acts 17:11). Importantly, this did not result in a rebuke: how dare you have the audacity to question an apostle! Instead, the Bereans are commended and described as noble for demonstrating due diligence. Biblical faith is never blind. It involves engaging your heart, mind and soul. Lean on God's revelation in the world and in his Word, and with his help you will learn to discern truth from error. Faith and reason work together as two sides of the same coin, and whenever we ignore reason and fall back on our feelings we leave ourselves vulnerable to making a serious mistake.

Faith to Stand

Faith is fundamental to Christianity, but some people say it is the amount of faith that really counts, implying that success in Christian living is directly proportionate to the measure of one's faith. This claim finds a comfortable home in the prosperity gospel, the idea that God wants you to get what you want as long as you have enough faith: you can expect to receive when you have faith to believe! This is a dangerous distortion of the biblical message, and like any effective deception it contains an element of truth. But it shifts the emphasis from God to us so that God becomes like a genie in a bottle—we can use him for our own ends as long as we rub him the right way. The Bible certainly encourages us to demonstrate faith and bring our requests to God (Lk 18:1-8), but we must temper every request, trusting him for the final outcome and asking that his will be done in every situation. We see this most powerfully in the life of Jesus Christ (Mt 26:39).

God asks for only a small amount of faith—just enough to trust—which contrasts the idea that God wants us to pump up our faith like we would blow up a balloon. When our focus is on how much faith we can generate by sheer determination, it means we have the power. Therefore we deserve the plaudits when we succeed (you made it!) or the criticism when we do not (you failed!). This damaging approach to faith leads to disappointment and dejection, and we need to distance ourselves from it. Jesus taught his disciples about faith, saying, "If you have faith as small as a mustard seed . . . nothing will be impossible for you" (Mt 17:20). Jesus drew a parallel between one of the smallest things lying on the ground and the amount of faith necessary to see God do great things.

When Sheryl and I moved into our first house we were delighted to get to know our neighbors across the street. Jim and his family were well-known and well-loved in the town, and his natural ability to bring a story to life meant our conversations were always memorable. As we got to know each other we started to talk about things that really matter, and I was curious about where Jim stood in relation to life and the big picture. Having grown up in the local church, Jim had a solid understanding of Christian belief, and one day I was able to talk to him about where he stood in relationship to God. Jim had the basic knowledge—he even had a simple faith—but he had never exercised that faith and personally made the decision to ask God for forgiveness and trust in Jesus Christ. But God was already at work in Jim's life, and he recognized that what he knew in his head he had never fully embraced in his heart. That day he was ready: to respond and take the step of faith to trust in Christ, beginning a relationship with God that would last forever.

Jim had just enough faith that day to take the step and commit his life to Jesus Christ, and Sheryl and I began to see God at work. Jim told us things were different when he went back to church. Listening to the Bible and the words of the songs, he would think, "I get it!" He looked at others in the congregation and wondered, "Do they get it?" It was like he was seeing with new eyes, and in a way he was since the Bible says a Christian is a new creation (2 Cor 5:21). As with any journey, the first step is crucial. Jim's new life started the moment he moved beyond religion about God to relationship with God. He did not have to pump up his faith to bring this about; he needed just enough faith to step out and reach out to God.

A wise man once said strong faith in a weak plank will get you wet but weak faith in a strong plank will get you across the river. If you need to cross a river, the crucial question is not how much faith you have but how strong is the plank. If the object of your faith is weak you can look forward to a big splash, even when you walk with confidence. If the object of your faith is strong you only need a little faith, enough to walk forward one small step at a time. God wants us to have faith in him, the kind that is reasonable and resonates with the real world, but all we need is enough to trust him, one step at a time. The Bible says that if we do this, we will see God at work in our lives in a wonderful way.[34]

Faith in Action

Because faith is generally misunderstood in our culture, we need to reclaim the foundation for faith. Some religions encourage blind faith, but the Christian worldview is anchored on more reasonable ground. That's why it's important to create a little distance between faith and feeling to reestablish the marriage between faith and reason. Christians who have been swayed by the culture may have secured their faith on their feelings, so we need to encourage a more balanced and biblical approach. Others have a deliberate agenda to undermine the credibility of Christian faith, and we need to be ready to offer a reasonable response. Christian faith is not out of touch with the real world; it draws strength and power from the fact that it resonates with the real world. But we need to be aware of people who elevate faith to the point that they try to use it to achieve personal success and prosperity. This is a false teaching ignorant of the biblical injunction: faith is about quality, not quantity, and it is where we place our faith that counts.

Summary
Faith is typically described as blind, particularly religious faith, but biblical faith is reasonable and resonates with the real world. Faith is influenced by feelings and feelings are influenced by faith, but we cannot afford to anchor our faith solely in our feelings.

Discussion
How would the people in your life describe faith? What would you say to help develop a balanced and biblical understanding?

Is there a time your faith stood strong under difficult circumstances? Recall the reasons why and think how these reasons could help and encourage others.

Recommended Reading
G. K. Chesterton. *The Everlasting Man.* San Francisco: Ignatius, 1993.
Ravi Zacharias. *Jesus Among Other Gods.* Nashville: W Publishing Group, 2000.

5

DOUBT

Be Prepared to Deal with It

*"You're a Christian—don't you
ever have doubts?"*

*"No. I can't afford to because doubt's
a slippery slope."*

"What do you mean?"

*"Well, if you open the door to doubt
it will destroy your faith."*

When two Jehovah's Witnesses came to my door I was prepared to have a meaningful conversation, but I also wanted to know if these ladies were as "open" as they wanted me to be. So I shared my passion for the truth, pointing out that I had many good reasons to believe that Christianity is true (and superior to the belief of Jehovah's Witnesses), but if I was wrong, I genuinely wanted to be steered back in the right direction. I asked these ladies if they felt the same way. One immediately said she was not wrong, so I clarified that I only wanted to confirm that she was open-minded enough to admit she could be mistaken. She refused to concede this, denying it was even possible that she could be wrong, and this conversation was over before it began.

There is little point trying to carry out a dialogue when one person is committed to delivering a monologue, so sadly the two ladies went on their way (next door). This was not a clever tactic I employed to avoid unwanted confrontation—although you are free to try it—but it does illustrate a fear many people have: that if you open the door to doubt it will destroy your faith.

The Danger of Doubt

While doubt can certainly be dangerous, I trust this chapter will help you avoid the popular rejoinder to difficult questions: "Jesus said it; I believe it; that settles it!" As a Christian I do not question anything Jesus said, since I have many reasons to believe he is the perfect Son of God who is the absolute authority on all matters, but I've always struggled with this retort. It makes it seem like Christianity has something to hide, a thought that struck me again when I heard actor and comedian Ricky Gervais share his own story during a 2009 television interview on Bravo's *Inside the Actor's Studio*.

As a young boy Gervais was captivated by Jesus Christ: "I loved Jesus, he was my Superhero! . . . And what I loved about Jesus was he was kind, and he was brave, and I thought he was amazing." However, Gervais began to doubt. One day his brother Bob questioned his childlike commitment. This did not upset Gervais. Significantly, he was more troubled by his mother's reaction: "[Bob asked me] 'Why do you believe in God?' and my Mum [said,] 'Bob! Shut up!' and I knew she had something to hide, and he was telling the truth. . . . I worked it out and I was an atheist in an hour." Ricky Gervais was only eight years old, but he knew his mother's look conveyed a message to his older brother: "Don't you dare open your mouth and open his eyes to the truth." Her refusal to allow Ricky to scratch the surface suggested that someone had something to hide.

Unfortunately, I don't know much more about the journey that led Ricky Gervais to outspoken atheism, although I would enjoy buying him lunch and finding out. I am always fascinated at the way people arrive at whatever worldview they espouse, and when someone has a story to tell or serious questions about the Christian worldview we need to be willing to listen. Then we must do our best to consider their position before respectfully sharing how Christianity helps us put the pieces together. Not that this is purely a mathematical exercise, and we should be prepared, like Gervais, to tell our own story. Seventeenth-century French scientist and mathematician Blaise Pascal said, "The heart has its reasons of which reason knows nothing,"[1] and we need to engage both heart and mind to make sense of it all. If someone raises serious doubts about the Christian worldview, rather than stuttering, "Jesus said it; I believe it; that settles it!" I prefer a modified version: "If Jesus truly said it, we will have good reason to believe it, the confidence to defend it and the opportunity to experience it. I believe he did and we do, and here's the reason why . . ."

Dealing with Doubt

It would be unfair to shine the spotlight solely on Ricky Gervais or Jehovah's Witnesses, since the difficulty of dealing with doubt applies to everyone and every worldview. Even the adamant atheist who claims to be "scientific" forgets that her attitude should be one of inductive inference. In other words, it is never case closed; one should always be open to correction and redirection when there is good reason to believe otherwise. Unfortunately, Christianity has its fair share of less-than-shining examples of how to deal with doubt, and many of doubt's fiercest critics operate in Christian circles. As Christians we need to stop and think why anyone should listen to what we have to say when we are unwilling to hear what they have to say. Only when truth is our goal will we be prepared to do whatever it takes to bring us closer to it, and when someone refuses to admit "I could be wrong," it shows that his or her mind is closed and the conversation is at an end.

Some Christians will visibly gag at the thought of speaking the words "I could be wrong." It sounds like we're raising the white flag of surrender about everything we hold most dear. However, this reveals a misunderstanding about the way we handle truth, build belief, anchor our faith and deal with doubt. The jigsaw reminds us that we can put the pieces together—enough to be confident about the big picture—and still admit that some things are missing and other parts don't seem to fit. Our knowledge is less than perfect, but when we are challenged by what we do not know we can return to what we do know to see if it's sufficient to deal with our doubt. It's not a sign of weakness to open your mouth and say, "I could be wrong." It could even be the key that opens the door to a meaningful conversation. When it does we have an opportunity to continue, "But let me tell you why I'm confident that this way of looking at the world is right."

Unfortunately many Christians fail to appreciate this and still consider doubt too hot to handle, so when I work with groups I deliberately tackle this "elephant in the room." However, due to the sensitivity of the subject I find it wise to take a more indirect approach. First I establish something innocuous that seems fairly certain and then introduce the element of doubt—for example, I call on a man who is proud to be a Scotsman and ask if it's possible that he was not born in Scotland. Like most Scots he rankles at this suggestion and perhaps refuses to consider it possible. So I return to the land of creative scenarios: maybe he was born south of the border in England, only raised in Scotland, and his parents have hidden this fact from him. I can push this as far as necessary to prove that it's at least possible. But as we established in chapter three, possibility is not synonymous with probability. Our Scottish friend can easily deal with doubt by falling back on his many good reasons to believe that he's a true Scot, and the whole experience ends up more edifying than terrifying.

Using this momentum, I could switch gears and take the same approach in conjunction with a deeply held Christian belief—I could ask a committed Christian if it's possible that Jesus did not rise from the dead. Once again the initial reaction may be shock and a resounding "No!" But I stick out my chin and say surely it's possible that Christian belief is founded on a falsehood. After all, the apostle Paul made the same point in his letter to the Corinthians: "If Christ has not been raised, our preaching is useless and so is your faith" (1 Cor 15:14). Paul's argument was to provide powerful reasons to believe that Jesus did rise again from the dead, showing us how to deal with doubt, but he does so by presenting the alternative as a logical possibility (with painful consequences).

Doubt can arise in anyone's mind at any time, and left alone it becomes corrosive, eroding the foundation of the Christian worldview. Indeed the word *doubt* comes from a Latin word meaning "to be in two minds," and that's why we need to be courageous and single-minded enough to bring our doubts into the open. As William Lane Craig has said, "A Christian who is thinking for himself will confront doubts; and doubt, if not properly dealt with, can be tremendously destructive of one's spiritual life."[2] Like being in the dentist's chair, we will experience some pain when we dig deep into the root cause of anything that threatens us, but dealing with doubt is necessary to prevent truth decay. It also allows us to establish a healthier (and stronger) foundation for the future.

Dealing with doubt often brings up sensitive issues, and we need to earn the right to talk about things that really matter. Indeed, when we have our own doubts we ought to use discretion before opening up and sharing what troubles us the most. However, it's important that Christians avoid the general attitude of having it all figured out without a shadow of doubt. This is not only disingenuous, it creates a false level of expectation in others so that when they cannot reach these dizzy heights they feel like their faith has failed and fallen short.

Opening the door to doubt seems like a dangerous step, and in many ways it is. When we are willing to scrutinize our worldview (or allow it to be scrutinized) we may not like what we see. However, we need to see our own personal doubt as an opportunity to reflect on the way we look at the world and to make sure we're living in the real world. A jigsaw guide is a great way to snap things into place, and when we are confident that we can see the big picture, we will be better prepared to deal with doubt. That is not to say we will fit everything together, as Os Guinness notes: "As believers we cannot always know why, but we can always know why we trust God who knows why, and that makes all the difference."[3]

The Danger of Dithering

If doubt can be used in such a positive way, why does it continue to get such bad press? One reason: doubt can be synonymous with dithering. Consider those who avoid committing to anything for fear of getting it wrong or making a mistake: "Well, I just don't know because you can never be sure." Sometimes hesitancy is a wise option (just ask any chess player), but sooner or later we have to commit to something and allow others to make their move and have their say. Constant dithering means we end up going nowhere, which is exhausting for us and frustrating for everyone concerned.

Doubt can also be used as a deliberate delay tactic. Returning to the chess analogy, a player may avoid making any move in an effort to delay the game and avoid defeat—even if it means no one wins. In life we see this when others refuse to take a position on anything, feigning a lack of assurance about everything. It's impossible to have a meaningful conversation when someone constantly interjects with "But what if you're wrong?" My daughter Moriah loves to ask the "But why?" question, and while this is an important developmental step at her age, it should not go on forever. Sooner or later we need to stand up for something. G. K. Chesterton said, "I am incurably convinced that the object of opening the mind, as of opening the mouth, is to shut it again on something solid."[4]

In chapter two we discussed the shortcomings of Cartesian certainty, the idea that you cannot be sure unless you are absolutely certain, and we need to respond to those who (indirectly) point to Descartes as a reason to dither and delay. No one is consistently skeptical of everything, and everyone overrides doubt and engages with the real world every time they step out of bed in the morning. Doubt can sound a necessary note of caution, but it should never be inflated or conflated to the detriment of nailing down something somewhere. Appreciate the difference between sincere skepticism and dangerous dithering and you are on the road to developing a healthy respect for doubt. It should never be automatically denigrated and described as a sign of weakness. Doubt can be respectable, biblical and compatible with confident belief.

The Benefit of Reflection

"The action of thought is excited by the irritation of doubt," according to Charles S. Pierce,[5] and when doubt is the expression of a question that encourages reflection, it's a good thing. It stimulates us to dig deeper and think deeper. It can represent a turning point, the kind illustrated in the blockbuster movie *The Matrix*. In this science-fiction fantasy, Neo, the main character, is a young man who senses a fundamental problem with the fabric of the universe. This is deeply troubling to him. Enter Morpheus, a man who understands what it is like to live with this kind of splinter in your mind. He offers to reveal the truth to Neo—and set him free. However, he warns Neo that once he has seen the big picture there will be no going back, even if he doesn't like what he sees. Morpheus presents Neo with a stark choice: swallow a blue pill and return to whatever illusion helps him cope with reality, or swallow a red pill and be willing to do whatever it takes to know the truth. Neo swallows the red pill.

The prospect of discovering a dangerous truth can unsettle us in the same way. Many people look at life and in essence decide to swallow the blue pill, retreating into whatever helps them avoid dealing with reality. The attraction of avoiding difficult questions is noted by Pascal: "Being unable to cure death, wretchedness and ignorance, men have decided, in order to be happy, not to think about such things."[6] Aldous Huxley was an English novelist and futurist who gave impetus to what we see in *The Matrix*—and what we see in life. His novel *Brave New World* describes a society that regularly pops the blue pill in the form of soma, a drug used to drown out sorrow and suppress all doubt, at least for a time.

Now—such is progress—the old men work, the old men copulate, the old men have no time, no leisure from pleasure, not a moment to sit down and think—or if ever by some unlucky chance such a crevice of time should yawn in the solid substance of their distractions, there is always soma, delicious soma, half a gramme for a half-holiday, a gramme for a weekend, two grammes for a trip to the gorgeous East, three for a dark eternity on the moon; returning whence they find themselves on the other side of the crevice, safe on the solid ground of their daily labour and distraction, scampering from feely to feely, from girl to pneumatic girl, from Electromagnetic golf course to . . .[7]

The real world is full of intoxicants and distractions that take our minds off the gnawing sense that there has to be something more than this. We don't even need to cross the threshold of our front doors to check out and check in to whatever virtual world takes our fancy. When real life seems less than palatable there is always the temptation to look elsewhere, and in the face of doubt or difficult questions, like Neo we face a choice: swallow the blue pill or the red pill. The blue pill comes in various guises and stands for whatever helps us avoid dealing with difficult questions, filling our life and emptying our mind. Alternately, like Neo, we can be willing to do what it takes to know the truth and choose the red pill. This requires the courage to face our fears. As Neo was warned, this is a difficult road. We may not like what we find, and when we begin this journey there is no going back.

Serious conversations reveal what kind of people we're dealing with: blue pill people or red pill people. Is someone resistant to life's difficult questions, or is he or she prepared to do whatever it takes to discover the truth? I had a conversation with a good friend who's not a Christian, and I was sharing about the day I spoke at the funeral of a young girl killed in a tragic accident. The girl was a Christian, which eased some of the pain of that difficult day, but it led me to talk about the fragility and uncertainty of life. I was interested to see how my friend dealt with these issues but rather than take the opportunity to dig deeper he wanted to change the subject: "Can't we talk about something else?"

Christianity is often described as a crutch to help weak people wobble their way through life, but it actually involves great courage: a willingness to deal with life's difficult questions. Some of the answers may be reassuring, and there's no shame in admitting that Christianity is a tremendous help and source of support, but others are deeply unsettling. If we were going to create an illusion that made life easier and more bearable, we would not end up with the Christian worldview. This is one of the good reasons to believe the testimony of the early disciples of Jesus. They proclaimed a message that brought them social separation and physical persecution, and some even went to their death defending it. Those who choose to follow Jesus Christ do not take the path of least resistance. In many ways they face what seems like an impossible journey, which is why the supernatural reality of Christian living makes others turn around in amazement.

Throughout history Christians have chosen the narrow road, and when non-Christians question the strength of character of those who embrace Christianity, I like to pose the question: "If you were to start living as a Christian, would it make your life easier or more difficult?" Believers become part of a wonderful community of faith, directly benefiting from the support and encouragement of others. But the thought of going into the workplace, classroom or home and telling people, "I'm a Christian!" makes some people shudder. It's a statement that makes others uncomfortable, and choosing to adopt a lifestyle that falls in line with biblical teaching threatens to turn our world upside-down. Christianity is not for the fainthearted, and it is the weak who wobble and walk away. The Christian life is more than we can handle and more than we can take credit for, but that's why it points to the power of God, not the power of us. God wanted it this way so he gets all the glory.

The Value of Humility
If the Christian life seems impossible, the hardest part is taking the first step, an act that requires great humility. If some atheists are to be believed, humbling ourselves before God undermines our self-respect and goes against the grain of human dignity. The late Christopher Hitchens, a writer and public speaker who wrote the book *God Is Not Great: How Religion Poisons Everything*, reviled the idea of adopting such a servile attitude.[8] Bowing the knee to someone else is not a prospect many will entertain, but it is a requirement for embracing Christ and the Christian worldview. It helps when we know to whom we bow the knee, and servitude finds its rightful place when we understand the character of God, since he is one (the only one) worth serving.

Ian Leitch is a Scottish evangelist and Bible teacher who has faithfully proclaimed the gospel for more than forty years. While Ian teaches around the world, he has developed a special love for the people of India. When we worked together in Scotland, he invited me to travel with him on one of his visits. I enjoyed visiting this wonderful country, and the trip was memorable in many

ways. One day we visited a family whom Ian and his wife Morag
have supported; with their help the family has been able to put the
children through school and live in a modest dwelling. As soon as
we arrived, this family could not stop serving us and taking care
of us. I was a stranger to them who had done nothing to deserve
this, yet they wanted to serve me as an act of gratitude for everything that Ian and Morag have done. This kind of natural out-
pouring of affection is one the Bible highlights as a right response
to God (Rom 12:1). To understand all that God has done for us is
to feel our knees start to crumble, and in the end a lack of servitude says more about us than the one we should serve.

Educator Howard Hendricks asks the question "Are you a big
godder or a little godder?" There is no doubt that a true grasp of
who God is and what he has done radically transforms our lives.
It seems increasingly popular to dismiss any systematic approach
to understanding the character of God, and so-called systematic
theology is often viewed as a dry and dusty discipline that fails to
connect with people today. I disagree. This negative reaction generally reflects the superficiality of a culture unwilling to spend the
time and effort digging deeper. The result is that many people are
missing out on the rich theological treasures God has made
available to us.

As a student at Moody Bible Institute I was excited to pore over
pages of mind-blowing descriptions of God's nature, explorations
of his attributes, discussions of the depth and richness of his
name, and examinations of his decrees. Robert Saucy is Distinguished Professor of Systematic Theology at Talbot School of Theology, and his book *The Church in God's Program* has become a
standard textbook in Bible colleges and seminaries all across
America. When I went on to study at Talbot I smiled my way
through Dr. Robert Saucy's class, not just because he has a wonderful sense of humor but because the wonder of God was welling
up within me. This is a natural reaction as we grow and become a

big godder. As we increase our knowledge of God—both who he is and what he has done—it naturally provokes a deeper sense of humility, respect and adoration toward him.

Christians ought to spend more time reflecting on the things that encourage spiritual conviction and intellectual motivation to bow our knee and give our all to God. Atheists, on the other hand, find it easier to describe God in misguided straw-man terms since "a little god" is easier to knock down. In 2008 I witnessed this firsthand while attending a debate between Christopher Hitchens and John Lennox at the Usher Hall in Edinburgh.[9] This grand setting in the heart of the Scottish capital focused on this question: "Should the new Europe adopt the New Atheism?" Lennox is an academic from Oxford University whose background in mathematics (and interest in science) have strengthened his belief in God, and together these disciplines provide a reasonable foundation for his Christian worldview. Hitchens was an outspoken atheist eager to publicize the evils of religion, as detailed in his book *God Is Not Great: How Religion Poisons Everything*.

Hitchens's opening statement was about the horrors perpetrated by religion throughout the world and throughout history. It was a curious way to launch a debate since Lennox warmly received it, pointing out that he generally agreed with it. Lennox was not there to defend "religion" as the solution to the problems of the human condition. Instead he was defending the truth and reasonableness of the Christian worldview. He also significantly underscored that atheism has nothing to offer the new Europe, especially in light of the fact that many of the greatest atrocities in twentieth-century old Europe were fueled by atheistic ideology.

When an atheist argues there is good reason to reject God, and certainly no reason to humble ourselves and bow the knee to God, we need to make sure we reject the usual caricatures and solidly defend a biblically balanced description of God. When people complain about the horrors of religion we can agree, since there is generally no debate about this. While clearing this up will not encourage belligerent atheists to put down their hammers, it can tap into what lies beneath. Many, like Hitchens, do not like how it feels to place themselves under the authority of someone else unless there is something in it for them. This should come as no surprise because we all lean in this direction, eager to remain on the throne of our own life, but a willingness to abdicate is necessary if God is going to take up rule in our lives. This obligation to God involves admitting that we have been going in the wrong direction and saying we are sorry, which only makes things more difficult and distasteful.

C. S. Lewis said, "It needs a good man to repent. And here comes the catch. Only a bad person needs to repent. . . . The worse you are the more you need it and the less you can do it."[10] None of us enjoy admitting we are wrong—about anything. However, Lewis reveals how we break this cycle and reach out to God. "Repentance . . . is not something God demands of you before He will take you back. . . . It is simply a description of what going back to him is like."[11] Saying we are sorry still puts us in a vulnerable position because what we do and say reflects how we look at the world, and changing the way we look at the world threatens what we do in the world. Worldviews run deep, which is why we often bleed when others are critical. Life is tightly woven around the way we see the world, and if we want to know what others really believe, we can stand back and watch how they live. As J. P. Moreland asserts, "Beliefs are the rails upon which our lives run. We almost always act according to what we really believe. It doesn't matter much what we say we believe or what we want others to think we believe. When the rubber meets the road, we act out our actual beliefs most of the time. That is why behavior is such a good indicator of a person's beliefs."[12]

Just as our beliefs about the big picture provide our template for reality, if we allow them to be reconfigured we will discover that many important things in life no longer fit. That is why dealing with doubt can change our outlook on life and turn our world upside-down. Many people will see this coming and resist it at all costs, but others will be prepared to pay the price and do whatever it takes to know the truth.

Openness to Correction

When we humble ourselves and say we are sorry, we admit that we are open to correction and redirection. When this becomes necessary the temptation is to soften the blow and avoid paying the full price. I'm sure that, like me, you've been reassured by another person brushing off an apology by saying, "Oh, it's nothing." We've become conditioned to say whatever will reassure people that they haven't really done anything wrong and don't really stand in need of correction. Consider an apology you've made recently (most of us will need to brush off a few cobwebs). This time imagine the other person looking directly into your eyes and saying, "It's true, you've done wrong, but I'm willing to forgive you." This doesn't really trigger a sense of gratitude; it provokes a negative reaction. "What do you mean I've done wrong?" We are generally not as open to correction as we would like to think.

When my sister Paula married her husband, Mark, I took the opportunity at the wedding to offer a few gifts designed to provoke memorable words of wisdom. These were not my own, thankfully, but gleaned from the truth and wisdom available throughout God's Word. One gift was a calculator. I gave it as a reminder that when you make a mistake, as is true in the middle of a long equation, you cannot keep going in the hope that things will eventually turn out right. You need to go back to the point where you got things wrong, put it right and carry on from there. The same is true in all relationships. C. S. Lewis remarked on this in *Mere Christianity*: "When I have started a sum the wrong way, the sooner I admit this and go back and start over again, the faster I shall get on."[13]

The difficulty of doing this in real life struck me when I watched a video of a discussion hosted by the Discovery Institute's Center for Science and Culture, an academic initiative that encourages research into Neo-Darwinian theory and debates the belief that life is ultimately the product of unguided forces. Michael Ruse was involved in this particular discussion, defending a Darwinian position, and he listened attentively to theistic arguments that threatened to undermine his beliefs. In spite of their rhetorical force, he said he was not prepared to leave his position and leap into something else without knowing what that "something else" was. This struck a chord with me based on what C. S. Lewis said, and I was moved to write to Dr. Ruse. I reminded him we are not locked in to a worldview found wanting, even if we have doubts about the competition. We can always return to the deliberation stage. Sometimes taking one step back is necessary to move two steps forward, and without going back to put things right there is no hope of finding the right answer. Dr. Ruse is known for being warm and winsome, and he was gracious enough to send me a friendly reply, although as far as I know he stopped short of accepting my proposal.

Michael Ruse was at least open to the possibility that he could be mistaken, but others are completely hostile to the suggestion, refusing to consider that they could stand in need of correction. This posture is incredibly damaging when we want to talk about things that really matter—it is one of the greatest obstacles to a meaningful conversation. It takes a humble spirit to admit you are wrong about anything, and one of the first steps toward embracing the Christian worldview is knowing that God is God and we are not. For many this is a bridge too far. Even when we experience the kind of sober moments that remind us we are broken on the inside and stand in need of correction, we are unlikely to acknowledge this or reveal it to anyone else.

Admitting that we're wrong would seem to weaken us, yet it is the first step on the road to experiencing freedom and forgiveness.

To illustrate this, I could point to the day Sheryl told me that something in our house had been damaged. It was a solid wooden elephant I'd brought back from India. The trunk had been broken, but Sheryl did not find the elephant sitting on the floor. It had been carefully placed back on the shelf. Realizing that someone was responsible, we were eager to find out what happened. Not to punish the person—what we wanted was an opportunity to forgive the person who brought this about. If Sophia or Moriah was involved, we did not want her carrying the weight of guilt on her shoulders. We wanted to give her the opportunity to acknowledge her mistake and receive the gift of our forgiveness.

Although we asked our children and our neighbor's children, we never did find out what happened to the elephant. But I make the point to draw a comparison. The sinking guilt that weighs us down in life can be lifted when we turn to God and ask for his forgiveness. It is an amazing experience to receive this gift, yet we will do almost anything to avoid the pain and shame. The tragedy is that when we do this we close ourselves off from the gift of forgiveness. Being open to correction is one of the toughest steps to take, but it's where the joy of knowing God's forgiveness begins.

Ready to Respond

If we are committed to knowing the truth we will be ready to deal with doubt and avoid the danger of dithering and delay. We will also appreciate the benefit of reflection, demonstrate humility and be open to correction. All are crucial milestones on the journey to making sense of the world, and while dealing with doubt comes at a cost, it is worth paying the price.

Doubt ought to be tackled head on, and the greatest danger is inaction. The first inklings of doubt may not overwhelm us or shake our foundation. Instead doubt slowly seeps into our minds and causes our hearts to grow heavy, enough so that our beliefs eventually sink without trace. Charles Darwin gives us a cele-

brated description of a slow erosion of faith in his autobiography:
"I gradually came to disbelieve in Christianity as divine revelation. . . . Disbelief crept over me at a very slow rate, but was at
last complete. The rate was so slow that I felt no distress, and have
never since doubted even for a single second that my conclusion
was correct."[14]

The reasonableness of the Christian faith can be presented and
its claim to be the truth defended, but we cannot "prove" Christianity in the sense all doubt will disappear. Lack of knowledge
always leaves room for doubt, and that's why some people argue
that the only choice is between blind belief or sliding skepticism.
The jigsaw demonstrates another way. We can acknowledge the
presence or possibility of doubt and still be confident that we
know the way the world is and ought to be. Remember that you
can be sure without being certain. You do not need every piece in
place to see the big picture, and when you encounter doubt you
can deal with it by falling back on the important things that do
snap into place.

It is important to break free from the fear of doubt by openly
expressing it. Everyone can appreciate what it's like to struggle
with doubt, regardless of what they believe, and Christians are
no different. In fact Christians often struggle with struggling
with doubt, hearing the echo of Jesus' words to Peter: "You of
little faith . . . why did you doubt?" (Mt 14:31). We are tempted to
deny doubt and sweep it under the carpet, closing our eyes to
anything that raises difficult questions. However, when doubt is
there, it's there, and God is big enough to help us handle it. He
wants us to lean on him and on others, living and growing in
community with other believers. The Bible is clear: walking
forward in obedience to him does not mean the complete absence of doubt (consider the lives of the Old Testament patri-
archs or the New Testament disciples), and every time doubt
raises its head we can overcome it.

The Joy of Overcoming

Dealing with doubt can radically change a person's life, as we witness in the life of Antony Flew. Flew was a man of great intellect who spent most of his life writing, speaking, debating and publishing reasons to believe that God did not exist. He was considered one of the U.K.'s (and the world's) banner atheists. However, over a lifetime of learning Flew became convinced that the complexity of the universe suggested an intelligent agent behind it. Using a kind of jigsaw guide to making sense of the world, he put enough pieces of the puzzle together to see the big picture. His commitment to pursuing the truth was greater than his dedication to atheism, and he was willing to humble himself and admit he had got it wrong.

Flew did not embrace the God of the Bible or Christianity, as some claimed at the time, but he did reasonably defend deism, the belief in an "absentee God" whose existence explained the complexity of the universe but who was not personally involved in the affairs of this world.[15] While this falls short of Christian theism—the belief in a personal God who is intimately involved in our lives—it is a huge leap from atheism. Flew demonstrated great humility to distance himself from his legacy, as well as the atheist community, and he suffered serious backlash both professionally and personally. Disgruntled atheists who could not challenge his reasons for defecting decided to question his character—Richard Dawkins caustically criticized Flew in *The God Delusion*. Flew provided a telling response:

> What is important . . . is not what Dawkins is saying about Flew, but what he is showing here about Dawkins. For if he had any interest in the truth of the matter of which he was making so much would surely have brought himself to write me a letter of enquiry. (When I received a torrent of enquiries after an account of my conversion to Deism . . . I managed . . . to reply to every letter). This whole business

makes it all too clear that Dawkins was not interested in the truth as such but is primarily concerned to discredit an ideological opponent by any means available.[16]

Many worldviews tempt us by granting a degree of flexibility, but the Christian worldview soberly admits the truth: the world does not conform to us—we must conform to it. That is why Christianity presents a threat to so many people. Most do not reject it because they doubt it can help us make sense of the world; they reject it after considering the cost of embracing it. As G. K. Chesterton said, "The Christian ideal has not been tried and found wanting; it has been found difficult and left untried."[17] You can doggedly pursue your own blinkered approach to reality or you can humble yourself and be willing to count the cost of doing whatever it takes to know and embrace the truth.

For those who still fear the danger of doubt, I empathize. I have gone through dark psychological tunnels in my life. There were days I contemplated the meaning of life and struggled to come to terms with the answers—or the lack of answers. At one point I wrote in my journal, "Life seems to promise so much but delivers so little. The belief that we can complete the puzzle and make sense of the world is slowly shattered when we discover so many pieces missing. I feel I have reached the end of this journey, dropped into a void where I can do no more. It is time to stop—it is time to shut everything out."[18] I was struggling to make sense of the world because my expectations did not match my experience as a Christian. It caused me great pain at the time, enough so that I was tempted to block everything out. Over time God gently brought me a more balanced and biblical outlook on life. He encouraged me to stop navel-gazing and turn my attention to the pieces of the puzzle that did fit and told me more about him.

I know the tremendous freedom that comes through expressing doubt, the joy of overcoming doubt and the passion to help others who are wrestling with doubt. This is a large part of what drives my life and the ministry of Reason Why International. Countless Christians have had the same experience, as Michael Phillips recounts in his biography of Scottish author George MacDonald:

> So joyous was the liberation of his own soul that he wanted to share the freeing message. . . . With this desire came a blossoming confidence in his authority to speak out what he believed. A bold enthusiasm sprang up within him that he might indeed make a difference in people's lives, that he might minister to others struggling with the same doubts he had overcome.[19]

Summary

When you are troubled by broken pieces of this world that do not seem to fit, fall back on the things that do snap into place and help you see the big picture. Left alone doubt can be a dangerous thing, but learn to deal with doubt and you will strengthen your belief and be uniquely prepared to help others.

Discussion

What about life seems to challenge your beliefs? How would you respond to others who are struggling too?

Do you find it difficult to admit the presence of doubt whenever it raises its head? If so, how could you deal with it next time around?

Recommended Reading

Os Guinness. *God in the Dark*. Wheaton, Ill.: Crossway, 1996.

Francis A. Schaeffer. *The God Who Is There*. Downers Grove, Ill.: InterVarsity Press, 1989.

6

THE BIG PICTURE

Be Prepared to Show It

*"If this is really the big picture, why does it
seem like most people don't see it?"*

"That's a good question."

"And what do you think is the answer?"

*"Well, I try to stop and think about the reasons
people don't see it. Many have never heard how Christianity
paints the big picture. Others have been exposed to particular pieces
of the puzzle and gone in another direction. Some just don't want
to talk about things that really matter. Then there are those
who have caught a true glimpse and decided
they don't like what they see."*

If the Christian worldview is true and represents the big
picture that helps us make sense of the world better than anything
else, it provokes a question: why don't more people see it? Why do
so many people seem to be missing the right pieces—and missing
the point? Any thinking Christian will ask this question more
than once, and we need to consider what is standing in the way.

Think of those you know who do not embrace the truth of the Christian worldview and ask yourself a question: why?

One of the simplest explanations is that many people have never heard or understood how to see the world from a Christian perspective. This is an incentive for Christians to take the message around the world; it is also an incentive for Christians to take the message next door. It's sad that so many people have no idea what the Bible says, but the silver lining can be that they're genuinely curious about the Christian message. I have spoken in many schools and found this to be true. It has taken only one generation to see the Bible marginalized and even removed from many schools, with the result that teenagers often have no idea about the Christian worldview. This encourages them to enroll in classes that deal with religion and philosophy just to learn how others handle life's ultimate questions. In many ways this is an exciting development, and Christians need to be prepared to handle the barrage of questions coming our way.

Another challenge is those people who think they know what Christianity says but who have misunderstood the message. These people have gone in another direction after experiencing a distorted image of the Christian worldview, often through hearing about the terrible things done by "Christians" or in the name of "Christianity." These accounts bear no resemblance to the life and teaching of Jesus Christ but they do leave a lasting impression, so we need to deconstruct where a worldview has gone wrong and put it right by putting the pieces back together.

For others the pain and suffering brought about by religion in general can be enough to dismiss all religious belief. When people assume all religions are the same and they have heard it all before, they are more likely to close the door on a conversation. I noticed an interesting comment on a Facebook page recently that captured what many people feel. A man used three words to describe his status regarding religion: "No! No! No!" Then there are those

who have seen the light and decided they do not like what they
see. Seeing the big picture is not sufficient for people to accept it,
and the cost of trusting in Jesus Christ and the Christian worldview
means many choose to walk away.

The jigsaw puzzle is a simple guide to making sense of the
world. It brings ultimate answers within reach so we can know
the truth, have good reasons to believe it, anchor our faith in the
real world and deal with doubt. These are important. However, we
can talk about things that really matter only with those who are
prepared to listen. Socrates famously said that "the unexamined
life is not worth living," yet there is no doubt that some people
have decided to treat this realm like Pandora's box: keep a lid on
it. The first step in sharing your faith is not trying to figure out all
the answers; it is finding out if someone is willing to ask the questions. When the door opens we need to be ready to talk about
things that really matter and have a conversation that counts.

A World of Worldviews

Among those who do not accept the Christian worldview are
people looking in the direction of another religion. Every religion
paints a picture of how life's broken pieces go together, and those
who follow one religion generally believe this is the best way to
make sense of the world. The Muslim will revere the Qur'an, the
Buddhist will hold to the four noble truths, and the Hindu will
respect the Vedas. These claims to revelation do not tell the whole
story in the same way the Bible tells us the beginning, the middle
and the end of human history, but they do make crucial comments
about life and ultimate meaning. Every religion, including Christianity, claims to describe the real world, so each ought to accom-
modate life's broken pieces. As a Christian I am convinced that the
biblical worldview is true, and for that reason it should make the
best sense of the world. It ought to have the explanatory scope and
explanatory power to handle life's deepest questions better than

the competition. You will find some truth in every religion and the common denominators are a good place to start interfaith dialogue, but we soon need to turn our attention to the critical things in other worldviews that do not snap into place.

In conversation with a Muslim. Islam teaches that we must earn God's love and favor by fully submitting to him and walking in obedience to his commands. Gulshan Esther was taught this as a young girl growing up in Pakistan, and while she was raised a Muslim, she later converted to Christianity. This was a dangerous thing to do—it is considered illegal and can bring the death penalty—and the decision came at great personal cost. She tells her story in the bestselling book *The Torn Veil*, at one point recalling a series of questions posed by her father that reflect important aspects of the Muslim mindset:

"Does Allah know all the actions you do on earth?"

"Yes, Allah knows all the actions I do on earth, both good and bad. He even knows my secret thoughts."

"What has Allah done for you?"

"Allah has created me and all the world. He loves and cherishes me. He will reward me in heaven for all my good actions and punish me in hell for all my evil deeds."

"How can you win the love of Allah?"

"I can win the love of Allah by complete submission to his will and obedience to his commands."[1]

Christians can agree with Muslims that we are broken people living in a broken world, but from there we take radically different directions. Islam teaches that we need to live a good life, at least one in which the good outweighs the bad, but if a holy God knows everything and judges us based on everything including our deepest thoughts, surely we will never be good enough. If this sounds like a problem, the greater issue is that Muslims have nowhere else to go, at least not in those countries where Islam is dominant and conversion to another religion is outlawed. The Qur'an simply encourages Muslims to do their best without knowing if they are ever going to be good enough to make it.

The Christian worldview is based on the Bible and seems to have a better grasp of the problem. It also puts the pieces together in a way that offers hope of finding a solution. The Bible teaches that we will never be good enough to win God's favor. Nonetheless God has loved us while we were unlovable. Indeed, we love God because he first loved us, and it is because he loves us that he was willing to send his son, Jesus Christ, into the world to die for us (1 Jn 4:9-10). If we are looking for a message of hope and assurance in this world we will not find it in Islam or any other religion that simply tells us to try harder. Christianity stands apart from them all and says our hope is not based on what we can do for God; it is based on humbling ourselves and accepting what God has done for us.

In conversation with a Buddhist. Buddhism teaches that there is more to life than this physical world and that we should pursue a path of peace, although when it charts our course it raises a number of questions. Ravi Zacharias addresses many of them in his book *The Lotus and the Cross*, using a fictional conversation between Jesus and Buddha to bring important issues into the open. Jesus asks Buddha the following question:

> You told them there is no God. Then you told them there is no self. You also told them there is no one to pray to. You told them there is no one to fear. You told them everything is only within themselves, even though those selves do not exist. You instructed them that their good deeds have to outweigh their bad deeds. You carved into their consciousness a huge debt. You gave them scores of rules to live by. You told

them all desire is to be cut off. You told them you would cease to be, and, when they have paid, they will cease to be. How can all this bring peace?[2]

To state that the problem and solution are within ourselves when those "selves" do not exist is like trying to jump out of a bottomless pit: every time you prepare to stand on something solid to propel yourself upward, you end up sinking farther down. Buddhists may be unshaken by this, at least in theory; however, in practice they contradict this by securing their everyday life on a firm foundation, living like real people in the real world.

The Christian worldview affirms that we are real people living in a real world, and we are encouraged to pray to a real God. The Bible (and our experience) confirm that desire can be selfish and destructive, but many desires are good and ought to be nurtured, not ignored. Christianity makes sense of promoting the good and resisting evil, not to bring things into balance, but to advance the former at the expense of the latter until God eventually returns to fix this broken world once and for all. In the meantime our goal is not to lose ourselves but to find ourselves. The Christian worldview reveals our place in this world and our purpose in life: to begin a personal relationship with the living God that will last forever.

In conversation with a Hindu. Hinduism is a worldview that understands the difficulties people face in this life; all the same it offers a solution that radically misses the mark. Rabindranath R. Maharaj was born in India, descended from a long line of Brahmin priests and trained to become a yogi. However, he became a Christian and wrote a book that highlights many of the weaknesses of a Hindu worldview.

More than a million people eke out a pitiful existence in the streets of [Calcutta] without even a mud hut to call home. . . . To live and die in such wretched, abject misery, and yet to be told that you are God and only need to "realize" it . . . and to be told that the running sores on your body, the gnawing hunger in your stomach, and the deeper emptiness in your soul are only *maya*, an illusion . . . could there be a more diabolical deception?[3]

India is a colorful country, and I have met many wonderful and generous people there. Nonetheless, the impact of the Hindu worldview is easy to see when you look at life on the street. The idea of karma and life as an illusion has become cool in the west, but India reminds us that it does not paint a pretty picture. Those who find themselves on the lower rungs of the karmic ladder are resigned to lives of abject poverty and misery.

Jesus Christ inspires those who follow him to reach out to the social outcasts with love and compassion because each person is made by God, for God and in the image of God. People are not God but they are made in God's image, so every person is stamped with absolute value and deserves our care and attention. That is why Christians have willingly spent their lives in the gutters of Calcutta.[4] Christian missionary movements throughout history have devoted themselves to sharing the gospel and improving general health and educating the masses around the world. Vishal Mangalwadi is an Indian author who wrote *The Book That Made Your World*. In it he recounts the positive impact of the Bible wherever it has been allowed to shape society and establish what it means to be a human being.[5] Countless universities and hospitals owe their existence to those who looked at the world from a biblical perspective, believing that the world's problems were real and they needed to do something about it. Christianity is not a matter of standing back and telling people to look within. Christianity calls us to come alongside—in the material world—and help those less fortunate than ourselves.

Shining the Light

During a visit to Hong Kong I enjoyed a conversation with a woman in a coffee shop. Sue described herself as a Buddhist, so I asked her the reason she believed in this religion. She answered, "My family are Buddhists . . . and I find that it helps me." I respected this and shared how my Christian faith was a help and support to me, but then I told her that my passion was to know the truth. This opened up a whole new conversation because suddenly we were talking about something above and beyond our personal preference. Sue seemed to see something different in me and in what I had to say about Christianity helping us make sense of the world. She was full of questions. I encouraged her to keep asking and pursuing the truth, and when it came time for me to go I left her with two challenges: to read Ravi Zacharias's book *Jesus Among Other Gods* and to visit a local church.[6] I was struck by what she said next: "You know, that's interesting. I have a friend who is a Christian, and she's already been inviting me to attend her church." I looked at her and smiled, recognizing that God was at work in this woman's life and that I had the honor of being a link in the chain of the greater work God was doing.

I sometimes illustrate the importance of getting alongside those who need to see and hear the Christian message by taking a match and striking it. If I am speaking to a group of people, first I try to switch off all the lights and tell people to imagine that we are in complete darkness, to the point that we cannot see our hands in front of our faces. Then I strike the match and ask, "What can you see?" The responses are what you would expect: "the match," "the flame," "your hand," "your face." I keep smiling and replying, "Yes, but what else?" Normally I exhaust the supply of answers (and matches) and leave people scratching their heads. This allows me to step in to reveal the answer I was looking for: the darkness! You need the light to see the light; that much is obvious. But you also need the light to see the darkness.

Jesus is called the light of the world, and every Christian is supernaturally enabled to reflect the light and likeness of Christ. This is a crucial part of communicating the truth of the Christian worldview. As if you were holding a small flame, others will see the light in your life—and the darkness in their own life. The Bible describes people living without Jesus Christ as being in the dark, but many people do not realize they're in the dark until they come into contact with the light. You could argue that people are never entirely in darkness, since the light of God's revelation is everywhere, but the longer they resist the light the easier it is to forget. The darkness can become comfortable and offer a degree of security, since without the light our lives look all right, and we convince ourselves that if there is a God—out there, somewhere— he would have no reason to turn us away.

I enjoy watching the popular television program *Inside the Actor's Studio* because it provides in-depth interviews with well-known movie actors. I must admit, though, that my favorite part is the last question posed to every interviewee: "If heaven exists, what would you like to hear God say when you arrive at the pearly gates?" While the word "like" reduces the question to the realm of wishful thinking, the vivid image of standing before God and seeing how your life measures up is still powerful enough to scratch the surface. Many guests are brave enough to reveal something important about the way they see God, see the world and see themselves. I have watched many episodes, but to my knowledge no one has ever suggested this: "Sure, I'd like God to give me a warm welcome, but if I'm honest, he'll probably tell me I don't deserve to be there." I do not want to point the finger at Hollywood actors because we could ask people on the street with the same result. We know we're not perfect, but we think we're better than most people—we could produce a list if necessary—and if heaven exists, we assume we'll be good enough to make it.

If someone does not need to be saved he does not need a Savior;

if someone is not lost she does not need to be found; if someone is not in the darkness he does not need to be brought into the light. Christian evangelist Billy Graham apparently said the hardest part of sharing the gospel is not getting people saved—it is getting people lost. People tend to think they are doing okay. Yet on rare occasions someone sees the light (and the darkness) and says, "You know, if heaven exists, then I'm in trouble." This is the first step toward understanding the good news. It is evidence that God is at work in a person's life (see Jn 16:5-11; Mt 5:14-16). When people acknowledge that they don't deserve heaven it actually brings them one step closer to getting there.

When Christians come alongside non-Christians and rub shoulders it allows others to see the light, to see the darkness, and to know the difference. Christian living is not natural; it is supernatural, and this gets people's attention. It provokes the kinds of questions for which the Christian worldview provides the answer. Jesus spent most of his time on earth interacting with ordinary people, and the religious types accused him of hanging out with the wrong kind of people (Mk 2:15-17; Lk 5:29-32). However, Jesus made it clear this was the reason he came: to help put broken people back together. He connected with those who desperately needed to hear what he had to say, and he communicated the truth without compromising his message. Every follower of Jesus has a responsibility to do the same, and every Christian should occasionally stop and ask this question: "When was the last time someone accused me of hanging out with the wrong kind of people?" There is nothing in our nature that shines, but when Jesus lives in us he shines through us, making us the light of the world.

Confidence in Our Credentials
Christian living sounds daunting and sharing our faith sounds intimidating, but a biblical perspective gives us confidence in our credentials. The Bible is full of wonderful examples of what an

ordinary person can accomplish in the hands of an extraordinary God. A person who commits his or her life to Jesus Christ is empowered by the Holy Spirit to reflect his likeness and share his message. This is not something we can take credit for, since God is the one who brings about a supernatural transformation, but we are also responsible to be sensitive to him, attentive to him, and obedient to do our best (Phil 2:12-13).

Despite this, it's tempting to look at people around us and wonder, "God, are you sure you can use me to reach them?" For reassurance we can turn to the apostle Paul. In the first century Paul went to Athens and preached one of the most dynamic gospel messages ever delivered in a crosscultural context. Some scholars question the effectiveness of his message, wondering about the lack of dynamic church growth seen as a result (where are First and Second Athenians in the New Testament?) but I prefer to leave the unknown in God's hands and marvel at what we do know: the gospel cut through great confusion and a number of people committed their lives to Jesus Christ—including one member of the Greek council. Paul used a jigsaw guide to making sense of the world, identifying important pieces of the puzzle and fitting them together so others could see the big picture, and I want to highlight one significant statement in this passage that is often overlooked:

> From one man he made every nation of men, that they should inhabit the whole earth; and he determined the times set for them and the exact places where they should live. God did this so that men would seek him and perhaps reach out for him and find him, though he is not far from each one of us. (Acts 17:26-27)

Paul tells his audience that the context of every human life is sovereignly determined by the one true God, and his purpose is to put each one of us in the best position to seek him, find him and reach out to him. That means that our circumstances are not incidental or accidental. God loves us so much that he will do what is necessary to open our eyes to the truth. If you are a Christian and someone was influential in your decision to follow Jesus Christ, this person was handpicked by God and placed alongside you. He or she could have lived at any time in history, been born into any family, or placed next door to anybody, but God chose this person to come alongside you: this was the best man or woman for the job with just the right credentials. If you are not a Christian, God wants to reach out to you, which is one reason you are reading this book.

God works with eternity in mind, and this shapes every detail of our lives. He will use the right people to reach out to us, and he will use us to reach out to the right people. Christians look at non-Christians in their life and know they could have lived at any time in history, been born into any family, or placed next door to anybody. The reality is that God chose them to live alongside us. When it comes to reaching out to the people around us, Christians have been handpicked by God as the best man or woman for the job with just the right credentials. Sometimes we shake our heads, convinced that some people in our lives are out of reach and that God would need to use an international evangelist like Billy Graham to speak to this person. God could have arranged for Billy Graham to grow up next door, but he did not—because he chose you! If you ever feel like your circumstances are not the right place to share your Christian faith, realize that if this were true God would have put you somewhere else. The circumstances of your life, wherever you are and whatever you do, are what you need to shine and to share. You have been divinely chosen for this task. When you have confidence in God you will have confidence in your credentials, and at that point you are ready to start asking the kinds of questions that will allow you to talk about things that really matter.

Asking the Question

When we know our responsibility is to connect and communicate the truth of the Christian worldview, it makes it easier when others start talking about significant things. Unfortunately, this tends to be the exception rather than the rule, as people are generally hesitant about raising big-picture issues. It doesn't mean they don't want to have the conversation, but it could be they need you to take the first step. The best way to do this is to ask a significant question and find out whether the door to a meaningful conversation is open or closed.

I enjoy playing soccer and my family would probably describe me as a "soccer nut." My wife rolls her eyes when she tells people I bought our son, Asher, a soccer ball on the day he was born, and I am not ashamed to tell people his first word was "Goal!" I have played soccer all my life, and when I attended Moody Bible Institute I played on Moody's 1994 national championship–winning team. I was even recognized as all-American, which makes me smile since I was born in Edinburgh. These opportunities helped me realize the power of sports when it comes to sharing your faith. Someone once said, "When you get bumped, what's inside spills out." When the character of Christ spills out after a bad tackle (or a bad decision), people pay attention. Sports is a wonderful way to connect, get respect and earn the right to talk about things that really matter.

After seminary Sheryl and I returned to Scotland, and when we settled in the Scottish borders she started unpacking and I started looking for a "football" team. I connected with a few local Christians and together we started a soccer club. For seven years we played every week in every weather, and while most of the guys who came along were not Christians, I would occasionally share something about Christianity. One summer we even handed out sports Bibles. However, the Christian angle was always low-key because most of the guys were there to play and not pray. I did not want to turn anyone away by turning this into a Bible club, but I did want to be within reach of those who were open to finding out more.

To know if the door to a meaningful conversation is open or closed, we need to be close enough to ask significant questions. We also need to be within reach so that others can hear what we say and see that we mean it. Carl played on our team and told me he was about to leave on a trip around the world, so I was keen to talk. I found out he had taken a sports Bible, so I asked if he had read it. Carl caught me by surprise when he told me he had taken it to work and was reading it during his lunch hour. I asked if he would like to get together to talk more, and we arranged a time (over an Indian meal) to talk about Christianity and how it can help us make sense of the world and see the big picture. Asking a significant question let me know the door was open to a meaningful conversation.

On a different day, however, another player let me know the door was closed. I was warming up and kicking around with John, talking a little about my faith and the work I do. I decided to ask if John wanted to get together over a cup of coffee. John is a wonderful guy and he had become a good friend, so I thought he may be interested in talking more. But he shrugged his shoulders and gave me a polite "thanks but no thanks." John told me he was happy with where he was at—with what he believed—and we never got to talk more about life and the big picture. Christians need to respect those who are not ready to hear some of the things we have to say. With patience and prayer there may come another day and another conversation.

When the door does open, there is a lot that needs to be said. We can often find common ground by recognizing that this world is in a mess, which leads to more questions: how did things get like this, and is there hope for the future? We are less likely to engage others if we start quoting chapter and verse from the Bible, and while our goal is unashamedly to share what the Bible has to say, we need to build a bridge into the conversation. Identify a few of life's broken pieces first, show how they fit together and share how this helps us make sense of the world. Turning our immediate attention away from God's supernatural revelation in his Word to focus on his natural revelation in the world may sound like taking one step back, but sometimes we need to go back to go forward.

A Question of Origins

To talk about things that really matter we need to start at the beginning, asking the question, "Where did it all come from—you know, the universe and everything?" If people raise another question, politely make note of it and promise to return to it, but take care of first things first. The question of origins immediately raises the God question, which presents a fork in the road: God exists or God does not exist. Many people try to sit on the fence on this. I often hear the sighing remark, "Well, people don't believe in God like they used to," as if God popped out of existence as a result of declining popularity. As if he were like Tinkerbell and needed people to believe in him or he would die. J. M. Barrie created Tinkerbell as a character in a children's story, but many see a supernatural God in the same way.

The question of God's existence deserves to be treated as an open question, but when you raise it you will see that many minds are already closed. We have already discussed this kind of anti-supernatural bias that assumes that God does not exist until he manages to prove otherwise. God is basically guilty (of not existing) until proven innocent (and found alive). If you dare say you believe God exists, you are immediately placed in the dock—or perhaps it is more accurate to say you are placed in the stocks—and others are free to throw as much mud as possible in the hope that something sticks. Curiously, those who hold a godless perspective often assume they are free from defending anything, subtly taking on the role of judge and jury.

Christians can accept these ground rules all too easily, taking on a wounded posture and believing that it's up to us to provide an explanation for everything—even questions people are not asking.

A healthy debate is not a one-sided mud-slinging contest; it is respectful dialogue that deals with an open question. Each side has something to declare and something to defend. The question is, does God exist? Belief that God exists results in theism; belief that God does not exist results in atheism.[7] Atheists can reject reasons to believe that God exists, but they must also provide reasons to believe that God does not exist. Otherwise they don't end up with atheism; they end up with agnosticism, a weaker claim asserting that people do not know or cannot know the answer to the God question. Agnostics withhold belief. But if we can put the pieces together to show there are good reasons to believe that God exists, they ought to be open to considering them. Atheists are responsible to demonstrate how the broken pieces of this world fit together and resemble naturalism. They need to provide good reasons to believe that God does not exist. Most atheists are good at throwing stones, but this is foolish when you live in a glass house. Many missiles they like to catapult toward Christianity bring their own worldview crashing down.

The idea of the God question being an open question takes a while to sink in because we have become so conditioned to think of naturalism as the default position. In reality, most people on earth don't buy it. It represents a worldview that doesn't fit life's broken pieces, and it fails to help us make sense of it all. A Christian should always be willing to say, "It's possible that God does not exist, but let me share some of the reasons why I believe he does." And we need to remind atheists that they have a responsibility to make the same concessions: "It's possible that God exists, but let me share some of the reasons why I believe he does not." Many prominent atheists pretend to concede this—Richard Dawkins has said he cannot be certain that God does not exist—but he also says it is as unlikely as believing in the Flying Spaghetti Monster.[8] This is a good example of the kind of empty rhetoric that writes a good headline but bears no resemblance to reality.

Billions of people around the world, today and throughout history, have strongly affirmed that the God of the Bible exists—never mind the billions more who affirm a basic belief in God. This belief is corroborated by evidence in the natural world, it resonates with claims about the supernatural world, and it continues to transform countless lives around the world. Theism is espoused by people in every country, culture and context—from no degrees to Ph.D.s—and it continues to stand strong as the overwhelming majority position in the world today. If Dawkins is looking for a "pasta in the sky" kind of belief, he would be better advised to do a little navel-gazing and fix his eyes on something closer to home. When someone refuses to seriously consider a competing worldview, it reveals a determination to protect a belief rather than pursue the truth. Many Christians have painfully wrestled with the possibility they have got it wrong on the God question. I have grappled with this too until the bell rang for the end of the round and I realized my belief was standing strong, and standing stronger. I am sure people would have more respect for Dawkins and his position if he were willing to squeeze into some spandex from time to time and spend a little more time in the ring.

Despite Dawkins's popularity, his books remind us that when you take the world and human experience at face value, you do not end up with atheism. His worldview is based on the unlikely outcome of climbing Mount Improbable[9] and overcoming the fact that "biology is the study of complicated things that give the appearance of having been designed for a purpose."[10] Atheism is at a distinct disadvantage when we take a common sense approach to making sense of it all, so atheists will often state the conclusion before considering the question: the case is closed on the God question unless theists can manage to pry it open. Christians should be ready to label this a closed-minded way to look at things and a lack of confidence to start from scratch and say, "Okay, does God exist?"

A Reason for Reason

If we are going to make sense of the world we need to understand that naturalism does not fit. It does not even provide rational justification for asking ultimate questions. With naturalism there is no basis for believing that human beings are rational; in fact, the most likely outcome is nonrationality. As we discussed in chapter one, when the human brain is the accidental byproduct of a cosmic explosion, there is no good reason to believe what it tells you is true, and there is every reason to believe what it tells you is not true. To illustrate, imagine that I came home one day and heard my wife tidying up in a hurry to get out the door, knocking over a game of Scrabble and spilling the letters on the floor. As I went to pick up the pieces, I noticed a few letters strung together: I H-A-T-E Y-O-U. This "discovery" would not disturb me. I would not conclude that my wife hated me, had left the house and was never coming back. These were the product of an accident so there was no reason to believe they were communicating the truth.

Contrast this with another imaginary day when I came home and realized Sheryl was in a hurry to get out of the door. She brushed past me as I entered the kitchen, and I glanced at the refrigerator door and smiled. I saw the letters: I L-O-V-E Y-O-U. Because we use these letters to send messages to one another, I would have reason to believe that this was the product of an intelligent agent, namely my wife. I could be wrong; these letters get jumbled from time to time, but my belief about how the message originated would give me good reason to believe it was true.

Two apparent messages: spilled Scrabble letters on the floor and magnetic letters on the refrigerator door. I would have good reason to believe the former was false and the latter was true, and it would all come down to the question of origin. There is good reason to believe one is accidental and the other is by design, and if our brains are the result of an accidental spillage of atoms there is no good reason to believe what our brains tell us is true. Take this one step further: there is every reason to believe what our brains tell us is not true. However, if our brains are the product of an intelligent agent, designed to help us engage with the world, there is good reason to believe what our brain tells us is true. Admittedly, our brains are fallible, but we can generally rely on them under normal circumstances. The explanation for God-given brains that let us down falls into the same category as everything else that is broken in this world: when people rebelled against God and became separated from God, this earth, our bodies and our relationships—with God and with each other—began to bear the hallmarks and pay the price (Rom 5:12; 8:19-22).

Understanding Free Will

Another important conversation raised in chapter four is the question of free will. Those who hold to naturalism have no way to explain it. There is no basis for free will according to this worldview, and if naturalism is true the result is determinism. When human beings are purely physical then our actions are the result of physics, biology and chemistry. They are generated by nature and stimulated by nurture, but we do not direct them in any way—they direct us. So the atheist (and the theist, on this view) will believe and do whatever his or her brain says to, something Richard Dawkins fails to concede and Ricky Gervais has yet to realize.

The bizarre outcome of this worldview is that whatever we say or do, nothing is up to us. This strikes most people as simply wrong. Despite the influence of physics, biology and chemistry (which we acknowledge), we know what it is to freely choose. Freedom is a powerful human experience, and it makes sense according to the Christian worldview. Human beings are made in the image of God, and each of us reflects the essence of divine personality: we have a mind to think, emotions to feel and a will to make decisions. Freedom is part of our supernatural makeup, and while there is no natural explanation, the Christian worldview provides a framework that allows us to snap this important piece into place. God did not have to create us with freedom. He could have determined our thoughts, words and actions to ensure that we would do everything the way he wanted us to. But this would be a world without love. God loves us and he created us to love him, and you cannot make someone love you no matter how powerful you are. Love that is determined, coerced or the result of manipulation is not real love. I sometimes illustrate this by talking about my daughter Moriah. I am bigger and stronger than she is, which is not a great claim considering she is only a young girl, but I could gather a group of people together to demonstrate how much she loves me. I could start shouting at her, shaking my fist and threatening her until she was willing to say, "I love you, Dad!" As the tears fell from her eyes and as she stuttered the words through quivering lips, I would have nothing to be proud of. In fact, I would have a lot to be ashamed of, and as an expression of "love" this would mean absolutely nothing.

Turn instead to a day when I am sitting at home reading the newspaper and Moriah bursts into the room. She runs and jumps on my lap, sending the paper flying everywhere, and throws her arms around me. She draws her face close to mine, looks directly into my eyes and gives me a kiss, saying, "I love you, Dad!" As a father, it does not get any better than this. This is real love, freely given, and it is amazing. What is more amazing is that God created us with freedom because he wants us to relate to him as his children. He could easily overpower us, but he chooses to wait on us to freely acknowledge him, and he delights when we draw near, saying, "I love you, Dad!"

God created human beings to reflect his likeness and to bring him glory. We do this by loving him, enjoying a relationship with him and living in obedience to him. This requires freedom but freedom comes with responsibility. When God created people he introduced them to his law and established what was within reach and what was out of bounds. Yet the forbidden fruit became the focus of attention until people decided to reject God, cross the line and turn the history of the world upside-down. This was no superficial infringement. It could not be remedied with a quick fix. This was the created rejecting the authority of the Creator with the intent to de-god God and take up rule for themselves.

This "great divorce" created a chasm between God and humanity, and from that day on people were born on the wrong side of the divide.[11] The Bible uses the word *sin* to refer to the fact that we have missed the mark and fallen short. Thomas Morris said, "Christian theology explains human beings broke free of a proper relationship to their Creator. This resulted in disharmony within, disharmony among fellow human beings, and disharmony with nature."[12] When sin entered the world it ruptured our relationships and ripped the heart out of what it means to be truly human. We inherited this fallen nature, passed down from generation to generation, and we see it on the news and in our lives. Our bias is to go the wrong way because something inside is broken and needs to be corrected. Some say, "If this broken world is what freedom brought, it would be better to have been born without it." Apparently not, since God created us with it, and he delights when people use it to reach out and ask him to start putting the broken pieces of their lives back together.

I know a young man in Chicago called Danny who is a remarkable example of this. He grew up in the inner city with a broken family, no direct father figure and pressure to fall into drugs, crime and local gangs. His context seemed to point him in one direction, making the end of his story inevitable, but the reality is radically different. Danny benefited from the strong influence of a remarkable grandmother, choosing to go against the flow and move in the right direction.

I want to underline two important things. The first is that we applaud Danny for his efforts. The *Chicago Tribune* ran a full-page feature on his life, celebrating his success at high school and on the basketball court. The newspaper could add another chapter now that Danny has graduated from college. We do not say, "Well, he simply did what he was programmed to do" or "What's the big deal—his environment pushed him to do it." We know Danny carried a significant degree of responsibility on his shoulders, and the fact that he went against the flow is even more impressive. This was a human being who faced the pressures of life and was able to rise above them to do the right thing.

The second thing I need to point out, and not least by any means, is the deeper reason for Danny's strength, determination and success. Sheryl and I got to know him as a young boy. He became our "little brother" when we were students at the Moody Bible Institute, and one day as we walked home from Moody Church Danny told us he wanted to become a Christian. We stopped right there on La Salle Boulevard and he prayed to trust in Jesus Christ. This decision brought him into a relationship with the living God that lasts to this day (and will last forever), and it has given him supernatural strength to live above and beyond what could naturally be expected.

G. K. Chesterton said, "A dead thing has to go with the stream and only a living thing can go against it."[13] Danny has experienced the reality of Christian living. When you can say, "Jesus, I believe you are the Son of God who died for me, taking my place and paying for everything that should separate me from God. Please forgive me, help me to follow you, and welcome me into your family," the Bible says something incredible happens. A person who is spiritually dead begins to experience spiritual life, something Jesus described as being born again (Jn 3:3). Sheryl and I keep in touch with Danny. One day I called and he was unavailable, but when his phone clicked on to his voicemail he still managed to make me smile. "Hi, sorry I'm unable to take your call. Leave a message and I'll get back to you. And remember, Jesus is the answer!"

The Problem of Evil

When we turn our attention to things in this world that point to God and the truth of the Christian worldview, one of the greatest obstacles we encounter is the problem of evil. It is a significant issue with no easy answers. However, every worldview faces the problem and needs to explain how we put the pieces together and make sense of it all.

When someone refers to this in conversation we immediately need to distinguish between those who are asking an objective question and those who are suffering from painful circumstances. When someone is hurting, it's often more effective to put your arm around their shoulder than try to provide reasonable answers. Yet there are times when we have the emotional distance to deal with the issue, and we need to begin by turning the discussion around. The problem of evil is a problem for everyone, and it is rare when someone fails to see that there are things wrong about this world and that it would be better if they were put right.

We should never tire of pointing out that naturalism has no justification for talking about things that really matter. According to a godless perspective there is no evil in the world—in other words, there is nothing that happens in the world that ought not to be. The world is just the way the world is. What you see is what you get, and what you get is natural. Friedrich Nietzsche understood the implications of this. He rejected belief in God and on this basis rejected absolute good and absolute evil. Nietzsche even disliked the terms "good" and "evil" because he believed they restrict us. In his view they stand in the way of evolutionary progress, preventing us from being all we can be, and we should not serve them—they should serve us.[14] In case Nietzsche is dismissed as an extremist, Michael Ruse has written about this in a more contemporary setting: "[Good and evil are] just an aid to survival and reproduction . . . and any deeper meaning is illusory."[15]

Naturalism claims there is no universal standard for the way things ought to be beyond the way things are, and we lose the capacity for making moral judgments because there is nothing above us to judge between us. We have no authority to describe particular actions as wrong; all we can say is we do not like them. We cannot change the world for the better; we can only make it different. This creates a tremendous sense of frustration and confusion in our society because deep down we do have a sense there is a way things ought to be. As Chesterton wrote, "[There is a] difference between giving the orange to a blind beggar and carefully placing the orange peel so that the beggar may fall and break his leg. Between these two things there is a difference of kind and not of degree."[16] The trouble is that many people lack the worldview to explain this or support it, so when they recognize things in this world as right and wrong, we have a great opportunity to show how this snaps into place in the context of the Christian worldview.[17]

If God does not exist then good and evil are just an illusion, a social convention or a matter of personal preference. However, if good and evil do exist then God must exist, and the Christian worldview is the only thing that helps us make sense of it all. Vishal Mangalwadi shared his journey to Christianity in *The Book That Made Your World*, saying, "The first chapters of the Bible . . . seemed to fit reality better than the intellectual options offered by my university or friends. I began to get excited about the Bible because it provided me with explanations. It made greater sense of who I was—a godlike person with a capacity to know, experience, and enjoy goodness, beauty, and truth."[18]

The Search for Meaning
Ultimate questions should never be automatically ruled out of reach, and a jigsaw guide brings us closer to seeing the big picture and finding the meaning of life. Every worldview has something to say about the meaning of life, and we have considered some of the disturbing consequences of naturalism, Islam, Buddhism and Hinduism. Naturalism has received a lot of attention on these

pages, and it can be vexing that a worldview that so radically misses the mark enjoys such great success in terms of cultural power and influence. Vexing but not surprising. The appeal of defining your life in a world without God (creating the illusion of autonomy) has great pulling power, and the spotlight rarely shines on the true consequences of Bertrand Russell's realism. When it comes to making sense of it all, atheists prefer to instill confidence in the troops by encouraging a more lighthearted (and short-sighted) approach. Douglas Adams is a good example of an atheist who winsomely discouraged us from trying to find the meaning of life or make sense of this world. He did this very creatively—and with a smile—when he wrote the popular book *The Hitchhiker's Guide to the Galaxy*.[19] While he is less forthright than Russell about the unsettling consequences of atheism, it is worth reflecting on some of the important things he had to say.

In his fictional story of intergalactic travelers, Adams includes the subplot of a supercomputer designed to find the ultimate answer to "life, the universe and everything." I often refer to this when I am speaking on the subject of making sense of the world, and it regularly raises a smile. Those unfamiliar with the story suddenly pay more attention, curious to know what this computer had to say, while others wait, ready for the moment Adams builds them up and lets them down. The computer eventually comes up with the answer "forty two," which only causes the reader to wonder: okay, so what is the ultimate question? The answer (or, should I say, the question) is a galactic anticlimax: "What is six times nine?" Obviously this does not tell us much. More troubling is the fact it does not even make sense—which is exactly Adams's point. His underlying argument throughout the book is that the universe does not make sense; at least it does not provide the kind of rational answers we are looking for. His less-than-helpful suggestion is a simple warning: "Don't panic!"

Despite some laughs along the way, we are left with the hollow outcome of a universal shaggy dog story, until we realize that

Adams has inadvertently reinforced some powerful realities that work against his worldview. The idea that life ultimately does not make sense generates deep anxiety. He acknowledges as much—hence the warning to stifle the panic that rises to the surface—and the book reminds us that we are wired for a world that does make sense. Also, it's no coincidence that Adams tantalizes us with a storyline that offers ultimate answers (even via a fictional super-computer) since he knows that this is enough to make people turn their heads—and turn the page. In the end naturalism is not natural.

It's difficult to override our predisposition toward the super-natural and the belief that life ought to make sense. Yet many persist in finding new ways to do so. Thomas Nagel is a professor of philosophy and law at New York University who has impressed many with his openness and honesty about the desire to hold on to his godless worldview with white knuckles: "I want atheism to be true and am made uneasy by the fact that some of the most in-telligent and well-informed people I know are religious believers. It isn't just that I don't believe in God and, naturally, hope that I'm right in my belief. It's that I hope there is no God! I don't want there to be a God; I don't want the universe to be like that."[20]

If people cannot deny the perseverance and popularity of a su-pernatural perspective that gives life meaning, they need to find some other way to avoid it. Rather than concede the need for some kind of religious realm that makes sense of our natural expe-rience—or admit their base preference and put their cards on the table, like Nagel—another unlikely escape route appears. The next claim is that self-deception must be key to human survival. The fact that people continue to expect real meaning in life has to be explained, but rather than rejecting naturalism (since it clearly does not fit) and returning to the philosophical drawing board, they blindly accept this predisposition as an evolutionary ad-vantage. Consider this statement from Daniel Dennett: "Whatever else religion is as a human phenomenon, it is a hugely costly endeavor, and evolutionary biology shows that nothing so costly just happens. Any such regular expenditure of time and energy has to be balanced by something of 'value' obtained, and the ultimate measure of evolutionary 'value' is fitness: the capacity to replicate more successfully than the competition does."[21]

Supernatural belief is described as the outworking of natural selection on the basis that it must bring some practical benefit to human beings. It must provide something that makes them fitter than the competition, otherwise the religious types would have been weeded out by now. Somehow our lives depend on the fact that we are brainwashed with the superficial belief that the world makes sense and life has meaning, even though deep down we know it does not. A kind of self-hypnosis is necessary for us to gloss over the futility of human existence. If this is true, it's worth asking why futility is so distasteful. Why have we not evolved to the point that we're prepared to high-five one another and grin about it?

G. K. Chesterton understood that naturalism suffers a crushing blow when we affirm life as absolutely valuable and meaningful and when we hold "a particular philosophy to the effect that life is better than death." Life is more than an accidental collocation of atoms; death is not simply a rearrangement of our chemical composition. Life is special—we appreciate this—and that's why Chesterton said we tend to think the cat is superior to the mouse, particularly when the cat has eaten the mouse. However, we need to encourage people to stand back and make sure their overarching worldview supports this belief. "If the mouse were a German pessimist mouse, he might not think that the cat had beaten him at all," Chesterton says. "He might think he had beaten the cat by getting to the grave first. Or he might feel that he had actually inflicted frightful punishment on the cat by keeping him alive."[22]

While our natural appreciation of the value of life is enough to dismiss naturalism, our expectation that life has meaning deals another fatal blow. The Christian worldview emerges as we put the broken pieces of life back together, and this is a good reason to switch to a top-down approach to see what else it has to say. Christians should never be ashamed to stand on the authority of the Bible as the inspired word of God, but beginning with God's natural revelation in the world helps us win an opportunity to share his Word, revealing the critical things we need to know from the mouth of the one who created it all.

We cannot rely on *The Hitchhiker's Guide to the Galaxy*, but we do have God's guidebook to the galaxy. This is a big deal, but Christians often take it for granted. Imagine a man running into the streets where you live, shouting, "They've found it! They've found it! The meaning of life, the question we've all been asking— 'What is life all about?' Well, it's been answered. It's true, and it's been written down in a book; you can even buy a copy. It tells us where we came from, why we're here and where we're going!" Most people would slowly edge away, deeply suspicious, but there would be a tinge of curiosity. Even the outside chance of getting insight into this question would encourage people to sneak a peek and perhaps whisper to the person next to them, "Where did he say you can get a copy?"

Unfortunately, the surest way to break the spell would be for the man to suddenly say, "Yes, and it's all in a book called the Bible." The Bible has been supernaturally provided, preserved and passed on to help us find the meaning of life, but most people do not see it that way.[23] It's often viewed as dry, dusty and irrelevant. And sadly some religious types read it and refer to it in a way that reinforces this stereotype. Christians need to appreciate what we have, God's guidebook to the galaxy, and know that it's our responsibility to communicate it in a way that reflects this wonderful reality. The Bible tells us the whole story of life—the beginning, middle and end—and when we know where we came from, we are ready to learn why we're here. My passion for helping others snap these pieces into place is the greatest joy in my life.

Reason Why International is a ministry that builds a reasonable platform for the truth and teaching of Christianity so we can share the good news of the life, death and resurrection of Jesus Christ. We may not get to this point in every conversation, yet the goal of every conversation is to get to this point. The crux of the matter is life and death—for today, for tomorrow and for eternity.

When you realize that critical pieces are starting to fit together, it's exciting to see something spectacular emerging. When you turn to the heart of the gospel, it is truly incredible. I have shared this message many times and seen many people respond and trust in Jesus Christ. The heart of the gospel is universal, and when the Holy Spirit helps people admit the basic problem and recognize Christ as the only solution, it's a dramatic moment indeed. Linda Zagzebski is one of America's foremost scholars in the philosophy of religion, and she said, "It is probably true that we ourselves do not really understand what we are doing until we can explain it from the beginning to someone who not only does not know any of the background literature but also does not know why anybody would care about such matters."[24] So this is our challenge: to put the pieces together, help others see the big picture and then share the gospel.

Sharing the Gospel

Here are the basic steps we should guide people through when we have the opportunity to share the gospel with them.

1. *Understanding the problem.* The Christian worldview establishes that God is good. We cannot even know what "good" is without him. He is the way things ought to be. His goodness is grounded in his character and is a natural reflection of his divine nature. God is good because he is—he can be no other way. God is holy. He is unique, set apart from everything else, and so far above and beyond us that we barely comprehend his wonder. God is the only thing in the universe that has always been and always

will be. Not only is God responsible for creating everything, he is responsible for holding it all together. God is personal. One of the most humbling revelations is that the almighty God who created the universe—and created us—relates to us personally and wants us to relate to him. He longs for us to reach out to him and enjoy a relationship with him that will last forever. This is all recorded in the opening pages of the Bible: a good God created good people and a good world. Yet this only provokes a question: so what went wrong? The answer is simple. We did.

God is the only standard that counts and we all fall short. Humanity bears collective responsibility for the decision to reject God, and each one of us suffers from a broken relationship with him. This supernatural separation is the essential problem of the human condition, and the solution does not start with us; it starts with God reaching down to us. The great divorce left us standing on the wrong side of the divide, but God has bridged the gap, which takes us to the heart of the gospel. Most religions agree that something is wrong with the world that needs to be put right, but Christianity stands alone as the only worldview that says there is nothing we can do to fix the problem.

2. *Appreciating the solution*. Most worldviews suggest that we can climb a ladder to success; most religions encourage us to open a spiritual bank account and try to remain in the black and keep out of the red. Christianity begins with some bad news: we cannot even reach the bottom rung on the ladder that takes us where we need to go, and we are all spiritually bankrupt. However, the wonderful message of Christianity is that while we could not reach up to God, he chose to reach down to us. He did this by sending his son, Jesus Christ, into the world, and Jesus was willing to leave the splendor of heaven to step into this broken world to fix the problem once and for all.

The Christian message revolves around the life, death and resurrection of Jesus Christ, but it can be difficult to appreciate what

Jesus did in the New Testament without knowing what God was doing in the Old Testament. When people originally became separated from God he still made a way for faithful individuals to draw near to him. God's law had been broken and justice required that something be done, so God introduced a sacrificial system. If people wanted to reach out to God, they could bring something precious, normally a valued part of their livestock or a proportion of the harvest, and sacrifice it by giving it up to God. This proved they were serious since each sacrifice came at great cost, and it was acceptable to God as something to cover the things they had done to offend him. It temporarily bridged the gap and maintained the relationship. It never dealt with the root of the problem, since people entered a cycle of sinning and sacrificing, but it was temporary by God's design. He introduced it to make provision for those who wanted to maintain a relationship with him until the time was right to put his ultimate plan into action.

We understand the need to make a wrong right as best we can. In fact, our entire legal system is based on trying to do what it takes to bring about justice. When someone is guilty of a serious crime, a judge is not at liberty to forget about it and set him or her free. There is a price to be paid and justice needs to be done. The Bible tells us that God always had a plan in place to repair the broken relationship that tore through the pages of human history, and he would ensure that justice was done. The Old Testament sacrifices provided a glimpse of what was to come—God was preparing to send his perfect son, Jesus Christ, into the world. Jesus would go to the cross and give his perfect life as the final sacrifice that would pay for the sins of the whole world once and for all. Jesus came to live among us to reveal the light and glory of God, but he was born to die, in a special sense, because his purpose was to give his life for each one of us.

Two thousand years ago Jesus of Nazareth was crucified, and the Bible tells us he died for the sins of the world. Jesus paid for everything we have done wrong, and when we trust in him he will forgive us and wipe away our sins forever. Jesus laid down his life for you and for me. He became our substitute, took our place, and through his death justice has been done and the price has been paid. Ravi Zacharias said, "Jesus does not offer to make bad people good but dead people alive."[25] So when Jesus rose from the dead, death was conquered and suddenly we had direct access to our heavenly Father through him in a relationship that will last forever.

3. Making a decision. Jesus Christ was willing to lay down his life for you and for me. We can do nothing to earn or deserve what Jesus has done; all we can do is accept the free gift of God's grace. It sounds simple, perhaps too good to be true, and it is not easy to take the next step. It involves humility: we need to be prepared to admit that we have a serious problem. It involves seeking forgiveness: we need to say we're sorry to God, but "sorry" is a hard word to say. It involves repentance: we need to be willing to turn our lives around and follow him, but many would rather go their own way. It involves a step of faith: we can put many pieces of the puzzle together and see the big picture, but there will always be some pieces missing. However, we can do enough to see the big picture, and when the Holy Spirit is at work in our lives we know we have a decision to make.

A story is told about a man called the Great Houdini who prepared to ride a bicycle across a cable suspended over Niagara Falls. A large crowd gathered to see the spectacle, so the Great Houdini turned his attention to them and asked, "Do you believe I can make it?" One group were in good spirits and shouted, "Yes, you can do it!" The Great Houdini steadied his gaze and looked directly at one young man: "And do you believe I can make it?" The young man was slightly unnerved, but as he was jostled by his friends he regained his composure. "Why yes, of course." At this point the Great Houdini reached down and stretched out his hand toward the man. This was enough to silence the crowd. "Good, then climb on board and come with me."

There is a difference between knowing something, saying something and doing something. The jigsaw is a wonderful tool to help us know the truth, Christians have a responsibility to speak the truth, and every person needs to do something about the truth. Jesus said we need to hear what he had to say—but it is not enough. Jesus said we need to understand what we have to do—but it is not enough. Jesus said we need to trust him—and that means people need to decide to climb on board. Our responsibility as Christians is to help others see the big picture, and when they do there will be a decision one way or the other. Some will decide they do not want to know, others will decide they do not like what they see, but some will be ready to respond. It is frustrating when people you love do not want to know. We are discouraged when friends and family decide they do not like what they see. Yet there is no greater joy than seeing someone make a decision to trust Christ, welcomed back into the family of God for all eternity.

Showing the Big Picture

My passion for writing this book and speaking to people of all ages and stages is that I am overwhelmingly convinced of the truth of the Christian worldview and its ability to make sense of the world. God's purpose in the world is to reflect his glory, and one of the most powerful ways he does this is by shining his light and life through the cracks of broken people. Everyone who trusts in the life, death and resurrection of Jesus Christ is restored into a right relationship with God, supernaturally indwelled by the Holy Spirit, and able to experience his power at work in their lives. This seals our relationship and makes it secure (2 Cor 1:21-22), but we are responsible to walk forward by faith. As we do this, he gets to work, transforming us from the inside out and putting the broken pieces back together (Phil 3:12-14).

This powerful message continues to reverberate around the world, and those who pretend to sound the death knell for Christianity have a problem. Christianity is not dead, dying or in decline. As Chesterton said, "It was supposed to have been withered up at last in the dry light of the Age of Reason; it was supposed to have disappeared ultimately in the earthquake of the Age of Revolution. Science explained it away, and it was still there. History disinterred it in the past, and it appeared suddenly in the future. Today it stands once more in our path, and even as we watch it, it grows."[26]

You can look at Africa, Asia or South America and see the rise and rise of Christianity, but you can also look at young people in North America and Europe to see the dissatisfaction of a dry and dusty naturalism that fails to meet our expectations or match our experience. There is a supernatural dynamic to life. It is necessary intellectually to make sense of the world, and it is crucial experientially to fill the void in our soul. While other religions try to put the pieces together, the Christian worldview fits and reveals the truth, and God wants ordinary Christians to share the good news. So the next time someone shrugs their shoulders and says, "Well, we can't really know because we'll never have all the answers," nod your head and smile. Then say, "That's true, but like doing a jigsaw puzzle you don't need every piece in place to see the big picture." Start putting the pieces together, and when you can make sense of the world you will be confident and prepared to share anywhere. This kind of experience has been captured powerfully by Chesterton, and it seems appropriate to return to him and close with these wise words:

> The grass seemed signalling to me with all its fingers at once; the crowded stars seemed bent upon being understood. The sun would make me see him if he rose a thousand times. The recurrences of the universe rose to the maddening rhythm of an incantation, and I began to see an idea. . . . I had always believed the world involved magic: now I thought that perhaps it involved a magician . . . that this world of ours has

some purpose; and if there is a purpose, there is a person. I had always felt life first as a story: and if there is a story there is a storyteller.[27]

Summary

There are reasons to believe that the Bible explains where we came from, why we are here and where we are going, and the truth of the Christian worldview provides a solid platform for sharing the gospel. The Bible says Christians are handpicked by God and strategically placed to share their faith with the people around them, so when you are tempted to question your ability you can have confidence in your credentials.

Discussion

If you are a Christian, are you rubbing shoulders regularly with non-Christians? What could you do to create opportunities to talk about things that really matter?

Think about other worldviews that miss the mark when it comes to making sense of the world, and consider how the Christian worldview addresses the same issues and helps us fit things together.

Recommended Reading

Thomas Morris. *Making Sense of It All.* Grand Rapids: Eerdmans, 1992.
James Sire. *The Universe Next Door.* 5th ed. Downers Grove, Ill.: InterVarsity Press, 2009.

ACKNOWLEDGMENTS

This book is like an iceberg in that what you see is heavily outweighed by what you do not see. So many people have played a part in seeing the dream of this book become a reality, and it is my joy to pay them the small honor of saying a public thank-you. While Sheryl and I draw strength from people around the world who encourage us and pray for us, unfortunately too many to mention, I want to recognize those whose direct support has allowed me to put my passion down on paper and see it published. I want to acknowledge the Reason Why U.K. board who were gracious and supportive of this project from the very beginning: Andy Bathgate, Lorimer Gray, David Dennis and Ryan Mc-Guinness. We also relied on those who regularly supported the ministry in this part of the world: Martin and Ann Allen, Mark and Paula Bowman, Norman and Helen Given, Elaine Kirk, Sam and Ruth Lee, Ian and Morag Leitch, Ryan and Jenna McGuinness, Soji and Sally Olakanpo, and Simon and Angela Wenham. There was also important support from Charlotte Baptist Chapel, the Souter Charitable Trust and Moody Bible Institute of the United Kingdom. Finally, thank you to the staff at Baxters coffee shop in Selkirk who graciously allowed me to spend many hours sitting on the premises and working on the book.

The board of Reason Why International seamlessly stepped in when the ministry relocated to the United States, and I am thankful to those who stand by me and serve with me: Doug Geivett, Eugene Johnson, Brian and Shari McAlpine, Lisa McKenzie and Howard Whaley. We lean heavily on our supporters in the U.S., and I could not have completed this book without the help of Brandon and Tammy Ballard, Brydon and Christina Bennett, Dan and Catherine Cooper, Paul and Wendy Dixon, Jim and Margaret Doll, Tim and Beth Donelli, Mills and Nancy Dyer, Jon and Diana Gauger, Peter and Becky Grant, Joe and Carol Harding, Roy and Kathy Harris, Betty Ann Johnson, Eugene Johnson, Sam Krikorian, Mark and Amy Long, Jordan and Jan Louie, Brian and Shari McAlpine, Ken and Lisa McKenzie, Ryan and Christy Peterson, Jeff and Caryn Silzer, Jim and Jean Warren, Bill and Norma Wayco, Howard and Lorraine Whaley, and Anthony and Jodi Zell. I also am deeply thankful to Eldon "Butch" Barkman, president of JAARS, for offering me the use of their facility to write—and drink coffee—and complete the first draft.

At one point this book was almost "put back on the shelf," and my dear friend Bruce Milne encouraged me to pick things up again. Bruce Milne and James Anderson provided valuable feedback on the first draft, and when I submitted the manuscript to IVP three anonymous referees provided comments that were also greatly helpful.

InterVarsity is a name I have long had great respect for. Indeed, much of my library bears its name. Therefore I would like to thank Andy Le Peau and Al Hsu for the opportunity to share my passion for the truth of the gospel on these printed pages. Al Hsu is the editor of this book and has been a delight to work with. Demonstrating great warmth, wisdom and sensitivity, he has taught me a lot, and this book is significantly improved as a result of his experience and input. I would also like to thank the marketing and design departments at IVP for their passion, creativity and commitment to work alongside me on this project.

Sheryl and I are blessed to have Christian families who constantly offer their love, support and encouragement. I want to thank my sister Paula, her husband Mark, and their two children, Sophie and Lewis. I also want to thank Sheryl's brother David, his wife Jan, and their four children, Lauren, Dean, Adrianna and Judah. Sheryl's parents, Gordon and Shirley Kooistra, have been a huge help in many ways, and I am deeply indebted to them for pouring their love and support into my life, marriage and ministry. My own parents, Alex and June McLellan, deserve a special mention for their unbelievable commitment to pray me through the process and across the finishing line. Their investment in my life is beyond measure, and I can only hope to mirror the love they have shown in my own family.

I could not write a book without a deep commitment from my wife and children, and they have overwhelmed me with their love and understanding. Counting the cost of Dad's preoccupation with "the book," Sophia, Moriah and Asher have been very gracious and kind in spite of their tender years. I trust God will bless them for their faithfulness. Sheryl has been amazing from the moment I suggested writing a book, and it is wonderful to have a wife who strikes the balance between allowing you to dream big dreams and keeping your feet on the ground. Sheryl knew this would place more responsibility on her shoulders, yet she stepped forward and was willing to help carry the burden. I dedicated this book to her not for sentimental reasons but to endorse the fact that I could not have accomplished it without her. Sheryl has been a constant source of encouragement, my primary proofreader and constant cheerleader, and I am blessed to have a beautiful wife who is also my best friend.

This book has been a team effort, yet there is no doubt who gets the last word. "Thank God" is often an empty phrase that spills from people's lips without too much thought, but it can also be the gasp of something supernatural that takes our breath away. The latter has been my experience. God spoke this universe into existence, holding everything together in his hand, and this same God cared enough to step into my circumstances on numerous occasions to support me as I wrote. What a mighty God we serve. I would not have completed this project without him, so I sign off by saying, "Thank you!" to my heavenly Father, Jesus my Lord and Savior, and the Holy Spirit for walking with me every step of the way.

NOTES

Introduction

[1]C. S. Lewis, *Mere Christianity* (New York: Scribner, 1952), p. 109.

[2]James W. Sire, *The Universe Next Door* (Downers Grove, Ill.: InterVarsity Press, 1988), p. 17.

[3]See Douglas Groothuis, *Christian Apologetics: A Comprehensive Case for Biblical Faith* (Downers Grove, Ill.: InterVarsity Press, 2011).

[4]"Modernizing the Case for God," *Time*, Monday, April 7, 1980.

[5]Alvin Plantinga, "Christian Life Partly Lived," in *Philosophers Who Believe*, ed. Kelly James Clark (Downers Grove, Ill.: InterVarsity Press, 1993), p. 69.

Chapter 1: Jigsaw

[1]Ravi Zacharias, *Jesus Among Other Gods* (Nashville: W Publishing Group, 2000), p. 128.

[2]Paul Little, *How to Give Away Your Faith*, 2nd ed. (Downers Grove, Ill.: InterVarsity Press, 1988), p. 22.

[3]G. K. Chesterton, *Orthodoxy* (Colorado Springs: Shaw, 2001), p. xxiii.

[4]Phillip E. Johnson, *Reason in the Balance* (Downers Grove, Ill.: InterVarsity Press, 1995), p. 204.

[5]A jigsaw guide to making sense of the world could be described as "exploratory particularism." See *Philosophical Foundations for a Christian Worldview*, ed. J. P. Moreland and William Lane Craig (Downers Grove, Ill.: InterVarsity Press, 2003), pp. 99-102.

[6]Terence Cuneo and René van Woudenberg, eds., *The Cambridge Companion to Thomas Reid* (Cambridge: Cambridge University Press, 2004), p. 4.

[7]Ibid., p. 11.

[8]J. P. Moreland, *Love Your God with All Your Mind* (Colorado Springs: NavPress, 1997), p. 153.

[9]Plato, "Knowledge and Virtue," in *Great Traditions in Ethics*, ed. Theodore Denise, Sheldon Peterfreund and Nicholas White (Belmont, Calif.: Wadsworth, 1999), p. 21.

[10]Terry Eagleton, *The Illusions of Postmodernism* (Malden, Mass.: Blackwell, 1997), p. 15.

[11]Thomas Morris, *Making Sense of It All* (Grand Rapids: Eerdmans, 1992), p. 186.

[12]Bertrand Russell, "Free Man's Worship," in *Why I Am not a Christian,* ed. Paul Edwards (New York: Simon and Schuster, 1957), p. 107.

[13]John Gray, *Straw Dogs*, 3rd ed. (London: Granta, 2003), p. 26.

[14]Ibid., p. 28.

[15]Ibid., p. xi.

[16]Chesterton, *Orthodoxy*, p. 43.

[17]Julian Baggini, *Atheism: A Very Short Introduction* (New York: Oxford University Press, 2003), p. 6.

[18]See John F. Post, "Naturalism," in *The Cambridge Dictionary of Philosophy*, ed. Robert Audi, 2nd ed. (New York: Cambridge University Press, 1999), p. 596.

[19]See John Lennox, *God's Undertaker: Has Science Buried God?* (Oxford: Lion, 2007), pp. 27-29.

[20]William Lane Craig, "Q&A with William Lane Craig No. 6: Definition of Atheism," Reasonable Faith, <www.reasonablefaith.org/definition-of-atheism>.

[21]See "Richard Dawkins celebrates a victory over creationists: Free schools that teach 'intelligent design' as science will lose funding," *The Observer*, January 14, 2012.

[22]Chesterton, *Orthodoxy*, p. 116.

[23]C. S. Lewis, *Mere Christianity* (New York: Scribner, 1952), p. 106.

[24]Francis A. Schaeffer, *How Should We Then Live?* (Wheaton, Ill.: Crossway, 1976), p. 19.

[25]John Locke, the seventeenth-century British philosopher, coined this term to describe the belief that the mind at birth is a blank tablet and the only input is ideas of sensation and reflection. See Nicholas P. Wolterstorff, "The Essay," in *The Cambridge Dictionary of Philosophy,* ed. Robert Audi, 2nd ed. (New York: Cambridge University Press, 1999), p. 506.

[26]R. C. Sproul, *The Consequences of Ideas* (Wheaton, Ill.: Crossway, 2000), p. 9.

[27]Schaeffer, *How Should We Then Live?* p. 165.

[28]Gray (quoting James Lovelock), *Straw Dogs*, p. 6.

[29]Friedrich Nietzsche, "The Transvaluation of Values," in *Ethical Theory: Classical and Contemporary Readings*, ed. Louis P. Pojman, 3rd ed. (Belmont, Calif.: Wadsworth, 1998), pp. 161-68.

[30]See John Toland, *Adolf Hitler* (New York: First Anchor, 1992), p. 544.

[31]Ibid., p. 226.

[32]Peter Singer, "All Animals Are Equal," in *Morality and Moral Controversies*, ed. John Arthur, 5th ed. (Upper Saddle River, N.J.: Prentice Hall, 1981), p. 134.

[33]I should clarify my position, and the Bible's teaching, that we should not pursue a taste test to choose whatever big picture is most to our liking. There are many who advocate this approach today (inside and outside the church), but my point is that we need to consider what resembles reality. Very often what we find out about the truth does not taste good.

[34]This presents one form of the cosmological argument for the existence of God.

[35]One of my opponents, a physics teacher, made this statement during a debate at the National Law Library in Edinburgh, Scotland, October 2009.

[36]Stephen Hawking, *A Brief History of Time* (New York: Bantam, 1998), p. 49.

[37]James Miller, *The Passion of Michel Focault* (Cambridge, Mass.: Harvard University Press, 1993), p. 185.

[38]G. K. Chesterton, *The Annotated Innocence of Father Brown* (New York: Dover, 1998), p. 35.

[39]Lewis, *Mere Christianity*, p. 5.

[40]See Don Richardson, *Peace Child* (Ventura, Calif.: Regal, 2005), and *Lords of the Earth* (Ventura, Calif.: Regal Books, 2008), as good examples of those standards that generally reflect a broken society in need of repair.

[41]I do not suggest this was merely a battle where reason prevailed, since greed and self-interest are generally immune to reason. Instead I would point you in the direction of the prayers of many godly people, over many years, and suggest that this outcome was ultimately won as a result of God's supernatural intervention.

[42]"The theistic conclusion is not logically coercive, but it can claim serious consideration as an intellectually satisfying understanding of what would otherwise be unintelligible good fortune." John Polkinghorne, *Belief in God in an Age of Science* (New Haven, Conn.: Yale University Press 1998), p. 10.

[43]The second law of thermodynamics, or the law of entropy, confirms that order tends toward disorder.

[44]The so-called New Atheists are a militant group of atheists dedicated to undermining belief in God and promoting a godless worldview in our culture. See Victor J. Stenger, *The New Atheism: Taking a Stand for Science and Reason* (New York: Prometheus, 2009).

[45]"The process that Darwin discovered . . . does all the work of explaining the means/ends economy of biological nature that shouts out 'purpose' or 'design' at us." Alex Rosenburg, "The Disenchanted Naturalist's Guide to Reality," On the Human: A Project of the National Humanities Center, <onthehuman.org/2009/11/the-disenchanted-naturalists-guide-to-reality>.

[46]Richard Dawkins, *The God Delusion* (London: Bantam Press, 2006), p. 135.

[47]Ibid., p. 140.

[48]Lennox, *God's Undertaker*, p. 69.

[49]Josh McDowell, *More Than a Carpenter* (Wheaton, Ill.: Living Books, 2009), p. 159.

[50]I use the word *heart* in the biblical sense—that is, it applies to the essence of the whole person, not simply the emotions.

[51]C. S. Lewis, *A Grief Observed* (New York: Harper One, 2001), p. 52.

[52]F. F. Bruce, *The New Testament Documents: Are They Reliable?* (Grand Rapids: Eerdmans, 1981), p. 76.

[53]Chesterton, *Orthodoxy*, p. 216.

Chapter 2: Truth

[1]Francis Schaeffer, *How Should We Then Live?* (Wheaton, Ill.: Crossway, 1976), p. 145.

[2]It's important to underline we need supernatural help to empower us to effectively share our faith, but we do not simply press autopilot and "leave it to the Holy Spirit."

[3]Frederick Coppleston, *A History of Western Philosophy* (New York: Doubleday, 1994), 4:64.

[4]J. L. Mackie, quoted by R. Douglas Geivett in *Evil and the Evidence for God* (Philadelphia: Temple University Press, 1993), p. 97.

[5]"The imperfections and narrow limits of human understanding [suggest that] almost all reasoning is there reduced to experience." Robert J. Fogelin, "Hume's Scepticism," in *The Cambridge Companion to Hume*, ed. David Fate Norton (Cambridge: Cambridge University Press, 1999), p. 90.

[6]Nicholas Rescher, *The Limits of Science* (Pittsburgh: University of Pittsburgh Press, 1999), p. 247.

[7]Methodological naturalism is the philosophy that drives scientism's investigation of a world where "everything is composed of natural entities" and "acceptable methods of justification and explanation are continuous, in some sense, with those of science." See John F. Post, "Naturalism," in *The Cambridge Dictionary of Philosophy*, ed. Robert Audi, 2nd ed. (New York: Cambridge University Press, 1999), p. 596.

[8]Henry F. Schaefer III, *Science and Christianity: Conflict or Coherence?* (Athens, Ga.: Apollos Trust, 2008).

[9]J. P. Moreland, *Christianity and the Nature of Science* (Grand Rapids: Baker, 1989), p. 103.

[10]Lawrence Cahoone, *From Modernism to Postmodernism: An Anthology*, ed. Lawrence Cahoone (Malden, Mass.: Blackwell, 1996), p. 2.

[11]NYtimes.com has articles on general noise pollution that stretch from the problems of barking dogs to heavy-metal drummers: Diane Cardwell, "Fight Between Bars and Neighbors Over Noise Heats Up," September 25, 2010; Sam Dolnick, "Heel. Sit. Whisper. Good Dog," February 3, 2010; Christine Haughney, "The Sounds of Drummers, Handled Gingerly—The Appraisal," April 19, 2011.

[12]William Lane Craig, "Politically Incorrect Salvation," in *Christian Apologetics in a Postmodern World*, ed. Timothy R. Phillips and Dennis L. Okholm (Downers Grove, Ill.: InterVarsity Press, 1995), p. 78.

[13]Joseph Natoli, *A Primer to Postmodernity* (Malden, Mass.: Blackwell, 1997), p. 129.

[14]James Sire, *The Universe Next Door,* 2nd ed. (Downers Grove, Ill.: InterVarsity Press, 1995), p. 97.

[15]J. Budziszewski, *Written on the Heart* (Downers Grove, Ill.: InterVarsity Press, 1997), p. 185.

[16]Stephen T. Davis, *God, Reason, and Theistic Proofs* (Edinburgh: Edinburgh University Press, 1997), p. 10.

[17]Frederick Suppe, "Becoming Michael," in *Philosophers Who Believe*, ed. Kelly James Clark (Downers Grove, Ill.: InterVarsity Press, 1993), p. 157.

[18]This image is borrowed from G. K. Chesterton, *Orthodoxy* (Colorado Springs: Shaw, 2001), p. 174.

[19]Schaeffer, *How Should We Then Live?* p. 146.

[20]R. C. Sproul, *The Consequences of Ideas* (Wheaton, Ill.: Crossway, 2000), p. 58.

[21]C. S. Lewis, *Surprised by Joy* (New York: Harcourt, Brace, 1995), p. 207.

[22]Peter Kreeft, "Why I Believe Jesus Is the Son of God," in *Why I Am a Christian*, ed. Norman L. Geisler and Paul K. Hoffman (Grand Rapids: Baker, 2001), p. 226.

[23]Phillip E. Johnson, *Reason in the Balance* (Downers Grove, Ill.: InterVarsity Press, 1995), p. 183.

[24]Richelle Thompson, "Dr. Laura's Order Under Fire: Local Foes Challenge Radio Host's Rhetoric," *The Cincinnati Enquirer*, Saturday, June 10, 2000.

[25]Chris Peck, "The Five-Minute Interview," *The Independent*, January 2008. Interestingly, the band Kill Boy Kill split up later the same year.

[26]Os Guinness, *God in the Dark* (Wheaton, Ill.: Crossway, 1996), p. 134.

[27]Thomas Morris, *Making Sense of It All* (Grand Rapids: Eerdmans, 1992), p. 17.

[28]Guinness, *God in the Dark*, p. 77.

Chapter 3: Belief

[1]Ravi Zacharias, *The Real Face of Atheism* (Grand Rapids: Baker, 2004), p. 59.

[2]Michael D. Lemonick, "The End," *Time*, June 25, 2001, p. 89.

[3]J. P. Moreland used this illustration during a Personal Foundations lab when I was a student at Talbot School of Theology in the fall of 2000.

[4]J. P. Moreland, *Love Your God with All Your Mind* (Colorado Springs: Nav-Press, 1997), p. 107.

[5]Richard Swinburne, *The Evolution of the Soul* (New York: Oxford University Press, 1986), p. 19.

[6]Thomas Morris, *Making Sense of It All* (Grand Rapids: Eerdmans, 1992), p. 123.

[7]Ibid., p. 127.

[8]Steven Davis, *God, Reason, and Theistic Proofs* (Edinburgh: Edinburgh University Press, 1997), p. 162.

[9]Introduction to the Book of Mormon (Salt Lake City, Utah, 1981), p. 1.

[10]This illustration reflects my encounter and the teaching in the Book of Mormon, but it does not rule out Mormons' offering a broader defense for the truth of their beliefs, and we need to be prepared to broaden our response.

[11]C. S. Lewis, *Surprised by Joy* (New York: Harcourt, Brace, 1955), p. 229.

Chapter 4: Faith

[1]Dr. Henry F. Schaefer III is one of the world's most distinguished chemists and has written a wonderful article on the Christian beliefs of many of the

early giants of the scientific method, including Francis Bacon, Johannes Kepler, Blaise Pascal, Robert Boyle and Isaac Newton. See Henry F. Schaefer III, "Scientists and Their Gods," Leadership U, <leaderu.com/offices/schaefer/docs/scientists.html >.

[2]Bertrand Russell, *Human Society in Ethics and Politics* (New York: Routledge, 2009), p. 209.

[3]Anselm, *Monologion and Proslogion*, trans. Thomas Williams (Indianapolis: Hackett Publishing, 1995), p. 10.

[4]Ravi Zacharias, *The Real Face of Atheism* (Grand Rapids: Baker, 2004), p. 112.

[5]Os Guinness, *God in the Dark* (Wheaton, Ill.: Crossway, 1996), p. 84.

[6]Phillip Johnson, *Reason in the Balance* (Downers Grove, Ill.: InterVarsity Press, 1995), p. 198.

[7]Richard Dawkins, *The God Delusion* (New York: Bantam, 2006), p. 45.

[8]Ibid., p. 1.

[9]Ricky Gervais made this announcement at the end of his presentation of the 2011 Golden Globe Awards. He has made similar comments while appearing on popular television programs *Inside the Actor's Studio* in 2009 and *The View* in 2011.

[10]The Bible teaches that God is absolutely sovereign, human beings are created with true freedom, and despite the apparent tension these views are compatible. For different ways to reconcile the problem see David Basinger and Randall Basinger, eds., *Predestination and Free Will: Four Views of Divine Sovereignty and Human Freedom* (Downers Grove, Ill.: InterVarsity Press, 1986).

[11]Richard Dawkins, *River Out of Eden* (New York: Basic, 1995), p. 133.

[12]The expression "ghost in the machine" was introduced by British philosopher Gilbert Ryle to describe the essence of what is called "mind-body dualism," where the soul (or mind) is believed to be distinct from the body. For more on this view see Brian P. McLaughlin, "Philosophy of Mind," in *The Cambridge Dictionary of Philosophy*, ed. Robert Audi, 2nd ed. (New York: Cambridge University Press, 1999), p. 684.

[13]Philosophers who want to retain free will but have no worldview to support it (or explain it) may resort to "epiphenomenalism: the doctrine that physical states cause mental states, but mental states do not cause anything." Ibid., p. 685.

[14]Alister McGrath and Joanna Collicutt McGrath, *The Dawkins Delusion?* (Downers Grove, Ill.: InterVarsity Press, 2007).

[15]See F. F. Bruce, *The New Testament Documents: Are They Reliable?* 6th ed. (Grand Rapids: Eerdmans, 1981).

[16]Michael Ruse, "Dawkins et al Bring Us into Disrepute," *The Guardian*, November 2, 2009, <www.guardian.co.uk/commentisfree/belief/2009/nov/02/atheism-dawkins-ruse>.

[17]Martin Beckford, "Richard Dawkins Branded 'Secularist Bigot' by Veteran Philosopher," *The Telegraph*, August 2, 2008, <www.telegraph.co.uk/science/

science-news/3348563/Richard-Dawkins-branded-secularist-bigot-by-veteran-philosopher.html>.

[18]Guinness, *God in the Dark*, p. 44.

[19]Mark Twain, *Following the Equator* (New York: Empire, 2011), p. 63.

[20]G. K. Chesterton, *Orthodoxy* (Colorado Springs: Shaw, 2001), p. 40.

[21]Debate between William Lane Craig and Peter Atkins, "What Is the Evidence for/Against the Existence of God?" Carter Presidential Center, Atlanta, Ga., April 3, 1998.

[22]William Lane Craig, *No Easy Answers* (Chicago: Moody Press, 1990), p. 35.

[23]John Gray, *Straw Dogs*, 3rd ed. (London: Granta, 2003), p. 28.

[24]C. S. Lewis, *Miracles* (New York: Touchstone, 1996), p. 24.

[25]John Polkinghorne, *Belief in God in an Age of Science* (New Haven, Conn.: Yale University Press, 1998), p. 124.

[26]Heinrich Dumoulin, *Zen Buddhism: A History*, trans. James W. Heisig and Paul Knitter (Bloomington, Ind.: World Wisdom, 2005), p. 169.

[27]See Paul Copan, ed., *Will the Real Jesus Please Stand Up? A Debate Between William Lane Craig and John Dominic Crossan* (Grand Rapids: Baker, 2001).

[28]Clarissa Ward, "Ex-Traffic Cop Says He's Jesus," ABC News, June 23, 2008, <abcnews.go.com/Travel/FaithMatters/story?id=5225539>.

[29]C. S. Lewis, *Mere Christianity* (New York: Scribner, 1952), p. 120.

[30]Ibid., p. 109.

[31]I am using the word *heard* in a very broad way that relates to God communicating in our lives and circumstances, not necessarily as a direct encounter with God's audible voice.

[32]Guinness, *God in the Dark*, p. 203.

[33]Ravi Zacharias, *Jesus Among Other Gods* (Nashville: W Publishing Group, 2000), p. 59.

[34]People sometimes quote Matthew 13:58 and point out Jesus did not do many miracles in Nazareth because of a lack of faith, but are they suggesting that Jesus was trying to heal people and it wasn't working? A better explanation is that lack of faith was reflected in the way people did not approach Jesus to be healed.

Chapter 5: Doubt

[1]Blaise Pascal, *Pensées* (New York: Penguin Classics, 2005), p. 127.

[2]William Lane Craig, *No Easy Answers* (Chicago: Moody Press, 1990), p. 30.

[3]Os Guinness, *God in the Dark* (Wheaton, Ill.: Crossway, 1996), p. 170.

[4]G. K. Chesterton, *The Autobiography of G. K. Chesterton* (San Francisco: Ignatius, 2006), p. 217.

[5]Charles S. Pierce, "How to Make Our Ideas Clear," in *From Modernism to Postmodernism: An Anthology*, ed. Lawrence Cahoone (Malden, Mass.: Blackwell, 1996), p. 145.

[6]Pascal, *Pensées*, p. 37.

[7]Aldous Huxley, *Brave New World* (New York: Harper Perennial, 2006), p. 37.

[8]"Why, if god was the creator of all things, were we supposed to 'praise' him so incessantly for doing what came to him naturally? This seemed servile, apart from anything else." Christopher Hitchens, *God Is Not Great: How Religion Poisons Everything* (New York: Twelve, 2007), p. 3.

[9]See <www.johnlennox.org> for information and resources.

[10]C. S. Lewis, *Mere Christianity* (New York: Scribner, 1952), p. 45.

[11]Ibid.

[12]J. P. Moreland, *Love Your God with All Your Mind* (Colorado Springs: Nav-Press, 1997), p. 73.

[13]Lewis, *Mere Christianity*, p. 22.

[14]Charles Darwin, *The Autobiography of Charles Darwin, 1869-1892* (London: Collins, 1958), pp. 86-87.

[15]William James Wainwright, "Deism," in *The Cambridge Dictionary of Philosophy*, ed. Robert Audi, 2nd ed. (New York: Cambridge University Press, 1999), p. 216.

[16]Antony Flew, "Book Reviews: The God Delusion," *Philosophia Christi* 10, no. 2 (2008): 473-74.

[17]G. K. Chesterton, *What's Wrong with the World* (New York: Empire, 2011), p. 19.

[18]These are reflections from my personal journal in 1991. I had recently recommitted my life to Christ but was struggling to establish a strong foundation for my faith. Two years later I was studying at Moody Bible Institute and adding weight to the anchor in my soul.

[19]Michael Phillips, *George MacDonald, A Biography* (Minneapolis: Bethany House, 2005), p. 141.

Chapter 6: The Big Picture

[1]Gulshan Esther and Thelma Sangster, *The Torn Veil* (Grand Rapids: Zondervan, 1984), p. 9.

[2]Ravi Zacharias, *The Lotus and the Cross: Jesus Talks with Buddha* (Colorado Springs: Multnomah, 2001), p. 70.

[3]Rabindranath R. Maharaj, *Death of a Guru* (London: Harvest House, 1986), p. 186.

[4]See Gregory Wolfe, *Malcolm Muggeridge: A Biography* (Wilmington, Del.: Intercollegiate Studies Institute, 2003), p. 371.

[5]Vishal Mangalwadi, *The Book That Made Your World* (Nashville: Thomas Nelson, 2011).

[6]Ravi Zacharias, *Jesus Among Other Gods* (Nashville: W Publishing Group, 2000).

[7]*Theism* generally refers to belief in God, but there are many God-type beliefs that would fit comfortably under this umbrella—e.g., polytheism, pantheism, etc.

[8]Richard Dawkins, *The God Delusion* (London: Bantam, 2006), p. 53.

[9]Ibid., p. 122.

[10]Richard Dawkins, *The Blind Watchmaker* (New York: Penguin, 2006), p. 1.

[11]C. S. Lewis's *The Great Divorce* (New York: HarperCollins, 2001) paints a dramatic picture of the consequences of this great separation.

[12]Thomas Morris, *Making Sense of It All* (Grand Rapids: Eerdmans, 1992), p. 143.

[13]G. K. Chesterton, *The Everlasting Man* (San Francisco: Ignatius, 2003), p. 256.

[14]Friedrich Nietzsche, *Beyond Good and Evil*, 1885, in *Basic Writings of Nietzsche*, trans. Walter Kaufmann (New York: Modern Library Edition, 2000), pp. 179-427.

[15]Michael Ruse, *The Darwinian Paradigm* (London: Routledge, 1989), pp. 268-69.

[16]Chesterton, *Everlasting Man*, pp. 107-8.

[17]Read C. S. Lewis's *The Problem of Pain* (New York: Touchstone, 1996) alongside his *A Grief Observed* (New York: HarperOne, 2001) for a powerful and balanced treatment on this difficult subject.

[18]Mangalwadi, *Book That Made Your World*, p. 53.

[19]Douglas Adams, *The Hitchhiker's Guide to the Galaxy* (New York: Del Rey, 2009).

[20]Thomas Nagel, *The Last Word* (New York: Oxford University Press, 1997), p. 130.

[21]Daniel C. Dennett, *Breaking the Spell: Religion as a Natural Phenomenon* (New York: Penguin, 2007), p. 69.

[22]G. K. Chesterton, *Orthodoxy* (Colorado Springs: Shaw, 2001), p. 153.

[23]Walter C. Kaiser Jr., *The Old Testament Documents: Are They Reliable and Relevant?* (Downers Grove, Ill.: InterVarsity Press, 2001); F. F. Bruce, *The New Testament Documents: Are They Reliable?* 6th ed. (Grand Rapids: Eerdmans, 1981).

[24]Linda Trinkaus Zagzebski, "Vocatio Philosophiae," in *Philosophers Who Believe,* ed. Kelly James Clark (Downers Grove, Ill.: InterVarsity Press, 1993), p. 253.

[25]Ravi Zacharias, *The Grand Weaver* (Grand Rapids: Zondervan, 2007), p. 82.

[26]Chesterton, *Everlasting Man*, p. 260.

[27]Chesterton, *Orthodoxy*, pp. 83, 85.